Insurance Law in Greece

Insurance Law in Greece

Ioannis K. Rokas
Kosmas K. Karanikolas

This book was originally published as a monograph in the International Encyclopaedia of Laws/Insurance Law.

Founding Editor: Roger Blanpain
General Editor: Frank Hendrickx
Volume Editor: Herman Cousy

Wolters Kluwer

Published by:
Kluwer Law International B.V.
PO Box 316
2400 AH Alphen aan den Rijn
The Netherlands
E-mail: lrs-sales@wolterskluwer.com
Website: www.wolterskluwer.com/en/solutions/kluwerlawinternational

Sold and distributed by:
Wolters Kluwer Legal & Regulatory U.S.
7201 McKinney Circle
Frederick, MD 21704
United States of America
E-mail: customer.service@wolterskluwer.com

ISBN 978-94-035-4791-6

e-Book: ISBN 978-94-035-4552-3
web-PDF: ISBN 978-94-035-4982-8

The Authors

Em. Prof. Dr Ioannis K. Rokas graduated from the Athens University Law School, Greece, in 1968 and became a member of the Athens Bar in 1971. He received a German Federal Republic scholarship (DAAD, 1971–1974) and obtained his Dr Jur. at the Free University of Berlin, Germany (January 1975) with the dissertation *Summenversicherung und Schadenersatz*, published by Duncker and Humblot, Band 22 of the series 'Schriften zum Wirtschaftsrecht', 1975.

He founded the law firm *IKRP Rokas & Partners* in 1977, now under the name 'Rokas law firm' with its offices in Athens, Belgrade, Bucharest, Podgorica, Prague, Sarajevo, Skopje, Sofia, Thessaloniki, Tirana and Zagreb.

He is an em. Professor of Business Law at the Athens University of Economics and Business, and a practising member of the Athens Bar.

He is the President h.c. of AIDA (International Insurance Law Association), member of AIDA Europe Committee and Chairman of the Greek Insurance Law Association. He has also participated in many scientific societies.

He has served as a member of the Project Group 'Restatement of European Insurance Contract Law' which produced the Principles of European Insurance Contract Law (PEICL). He has been the Reporter and Chairman of the Drafting Committee of the Greek Insurance Contract Act (ICA) no. 2496/1997. He has also participated in many Greek Drafting Committees on Insurance and Commercial Law Acts.

He has been an academic advisor to the Insurance Commissioner of Greece, and he has participated as a consultant in European Union (EU) that funded projects awarded to his Law Firm on Insurance Law and Regulation issues in Russia and SE Europe countries.

He is co-editor of the Greek quarterly *Commercial Law Review* established in 1950.

He has published many scientific articles in Greek and non-Greek law reviews, essays in honour, court decision commentaries, monographs, books for students on insurance, maritime and other topics of commercial law.

A selected bibliography on insurance law issues can be found at the end of this monograph.

The Authors

Kosmas N. Karanikolas graduated from Athens University Law School, Greece, in 2016 and obtained an LLM in Commercial Law, with specialization in Maritime & Transport Law from the Erasmus University of Rotterdam in 2017. He became a member of the Athens Bar Association in 2018 as a trainee lawyer and was admitted to the Bar in 2020. He is currently an associate lawyer at *Rokas* Law Firm (Athens), engaging in the provision of mainly advisory legal services as well as in legal research related to insurance disputes (insurance contract law, distribution of insurance products, supervision of insurance undertakings and companies' regulatory compliance) as well as company transformations (mergers and acquisitions) and energy law. He has also been collaborating since 2018 with the scientific journal *Commercial Law Review (EEmpD)*, where he regularly publishes critical remarks on recent court decisions.

Table of Contents

Table of Contents

List of Abbreviations

AII	Ancillary Insurance Intermediary
CPML	Code of Private Maritime Law
dwt	Dead weight Tonnage
EC	European Community
EEA	European Economic Area
ELGA	(Organismós) Ellinikón Georgikón Asfaliseon – the Organization of Greek Agricultural Insurance
EU	European Union
ICA	Insurance Contract Act
IDD	Insurance Distribution Directive
Leg.	Legislative
MTPL	Motor Vehicle Third-Party Liability
P&I	Protection and Indemnity
PAC	Private Aviation Code
RAS	Riunione Adriatica di Sicurta
SA	Société Anonyme
SDRs	Special Drawing Rights

List of Abbreviations

Preface

In light of the recent developments and the latest amendments of European Union (EU) Directives and Greek law, as well as in order to align the present monograph with the latest socio-economic developments in Greece, a new updated edition of the Hellenic Insurance Law was considered necessary. The present edition is aimed at the provision of a brief, fully updated, comprehensive presentation of the contemporary insurance law as is in force in Greece.

Acknowledgement

I wish to warmly thank Kosmas Karanikolas, LLM, my colleague at *Rokas* Law firm, for the updated information throughout the amendment of this edition.

Acknowledgement

General Introduction

§1. General Background Information

I. Country's General Information

1. Greece, officially the Hellenic Republic, is a country in south-eastern Europe. Greece has land borders with Albania, North Macedonia and Bulgaria to the north and Turkey to the east. The Aegean Sea lies to the east of mainland Greece, the Ionian Sea to the west and the Mediterranean Sea to the south. Greece has the twelfth longest coastline in the world (about 13,676 kilometres), which features a vast number of islands (approximately 1,400, of which 227 are inhabited), including Crete, the Dodecanese, the Cyclades and the Ionian Islands, among others.

Modern Greece traces its roots to the civilization of ancient Greece that extended from Epirus to Thrace and from Macedonia to Crete, including Peloponnesus, Mainland, the Aegean and the Ionian Islands. Greece is considered the birthplace of democracy, philosophy, the Olympic Games, major scientific and mathematical principles and drama. This legacy is partly reflected in the seventeen UNESCO World Heritage Sites located in Greece, ranking Greece 7th in Europe and 13th in the world.

The modern Greek state was established in 1821 when the first Constitution was adopted following the Greek War of Independence, and in 1830 the sovereignty of Greece was confirmed in the London Protocol.

A developed country with an advanced, high-income economy and very high standards of living, Greece has been a member of the European Union (EU) since 1981 and the Eurozone since 2001, North Atlantic Treaty Organization since 1952 and the European Space Agency since 2005. It is also a founding member of the United Nations and the Organisation for Economic Co-operation and Development.

II. Political System

2. Greece is a 'presidential, parliamentary democracy'. This political system is safeguarded by Article 1 of the Greek Constitution, an article which cannot be amended by any legislative procedure.

Democracy is a particularly loaded word in Greek politics, where the effects of the civil war, which followed the Second World War and lasted until 1949, as well as those of the military dictatorship of 1967–1974, can still be felt. Although Greece has had its full share of political upheaval, it seems unable to shake off its past history. Consequently, the political scene was determined for more than three decades (1974–2010) by the electorate's clan-like allegiance to one of the two dominant political parties. However, since the recent government debt crisis, party politics moved into a new phase. Several political parties have managed to enter into Greek Parliament since 2012, albeit parliamentary representation of some of them has proven rather meteoric, resulting in the weakening of the two dominant political parties, the centre-right New Democracy and the centre-left PASOK. The elections of 7 July 2019, though, marked the reinstatement of the central-right New Democracy in the administration, displacing the originally leftist and gradually moving towards social democracy SYRIZA that was running the country since January 2015 along with the minor conservative party ANEL which lost all its seats in the Parliament.

3. The Head of State is the President of the Republic, who is elected by the Parliament for a five-year term. On 13 March 2020, judge Aikateríni Sakellaropoulou, formerly Head of the Greek Council of the State (the country's Supreme Administrative Court), became the first woman to be elected as President of the Republic, receiving 261 votes out of the 300 members of the Parliament.

The Constitution provides that State Authority is divided into three separate powers: the legislative, the executive and the judiciary. However, the President, who has controlling powers over the Government and safeguards the political system, shares the legislative function with the Parliament and the executive with the Government. The President's legislative powers consist of his right to issue Presidential Decrees – which must also be signed by the competent Minister, who also bears the responsibility of their issue – and to promulgate the bills passed by the Parliament. As for his executive powers, these were severely limited after the constitutional amendment of 1986.

4. The Government consists of the Council of Ministers, which is accountable to the Parliament since it relies on the Parliament's vote of confidence and is headed by the Prime Minister. The Parliament consists of one chamber with three hundred members. These are elected for a four-year term. The members of the Parliament are directly elected, whereas the President of the Republic is elected by the Parliament.

5. The administration is divided into central and decentralized or local administration. The central government is divided into Ministries. The Minister is politically accountable to the Parliament and the Prime Minister.

Regional and municipal authorities enjoy decision-making powers within their region or municipality. The country is divided into 7 decentralized administrations, 13 regions and 332 municipalities. The regions and the municipalities are self-administered legal persons; i.e., their representatives are elected through direct vote. The municipalities are divided into municipal units and the latter into local communities. The regions are divided into regional units. One (in the case of Attica), two or more regions constitute the decentralized administration.

6. Greek politics are very lively. Political parties intervene in many facets of everyday life. It has been observed that political considerations have been the main criteria for the management and decision-making of state-owned undertakings in the past. Even in the purely private sector, decisions of significant economic interest are not independent of political factors. Political parties often influence decisions taken by trade unions.

7. Greece has always been a market economy. State Supervision of companies and businesses, in general, is restricted to the legitimacy of transactions and includes very limited intervention in matters of commercial policy.

8. The Constitution contains certain favourable provisions for third countries' foreign capital invested in Greece. These provisions facilitate the re-export of capital, interest, etc.

Article 28 of the Constitution provides that 'generally recognised rules of international law, as well as international conventions after their ratification shall constitute an integral part of Greek domestic law and shall prevail over any existing or future contrary legislative provision'. The same article further provides that under certain circumstances and upon a treaty or convention, it is possible for certain powers to be bestowed to international organizations and that national sovereignty may be restricted accordingly.

III. Commerce and Industry

9. The history of Greek commerce goes a long way back, even though the industry in Greece has not yet reached the level of other Western industrial countries. The majority of Greek commercial companies active in trade and industry are small or medium sized and still often family run.

Greek industry is in need of further modernization; however, it should be underlined that a limited number of industries have shown remarkable growth and innovation in the last years and have become global players for the first time in the Greek history.

The Greek textile industry (spinning and weaving, etc.), as well as the cement industry, is still an important sector, with a considerable market share in the EU, while food and beverages are another major component of exports which is rapidly and continuously growing. Tourism, the so-called heavy industry, is another significant source of income with great potential for further development, albeit the Covid-19 pandemic caused an unprecedented – yet likely temporary – decrement in tourist arrivals. Statistical data show that in 2019 alone, around 31.3 million tourists visited Greece, while in 2020 the relevant figure was confined to 7.3 million tourists, diminishing by 76.5%. During the first seven months of 2021, 4.5 million tourists had already visited Greece, implying tentative signs of recovery of the touristic sector, although this figure remains significantly decreased compared to 2019.

10. Owing to the outbreak of the pandemic, the upward trend of exports from Greece was reversed in 2020 as their volume plummeted by 21.7% in comparison with 2019, while provisional data for the second trimester of 2021 indicate a significant increment by 25.1% in comparison with the corresponding period of 2020. The destination of the majority of Greece's exports is the EU Member States. The problems facing Greek exporters are related to the high labour cost, which harms the competitiveness of the end product and the still existing lack of exporting culture of the Greek economy. However, labour wages are one of the main objects and instruments employed by the Greek Government in order to boost the competitiveness of the country in the present economic circumstances.

11. The development of Greek commerce is notable. The Greek economy includes a large transport sector, especially as regards maritime transport. Greek shipping has ranked among the most important in the world for many years. It currently holds the first position in the world for owned tonnage.

According to the Greek Shipowners' Union Annual Report 2019–2020, Greek interests control the largest percentage of merchant fleet in the world for total deadweight tonnage (dwt), which equates to 20.67%. Additionally, they represent 54.28% of all of the EU's dwt. They also control 32.64% of the world's crude oil tankers' fleet, 21.70% of the world's dry bulk carriers' fleet and 15.14% of the world's chemical and products tankers' fleet (in dwt). At the beginning of 2020, Greek interests also had on order 128 vessels (tankers, bulk carriers, containerships, etc.) corresponding to 25.38% (in terms of tonnage) of the ordered oil tankers, as well as 27.26% (in terms of tonnage) of the ordered LNG/LPG tankers.

IV. Financial Institutions

12. The banking sector displays an obvious tendency towards internationalization but has been affected by the recent Greek sovereign debt crisis.

13. During the decade 2000–2010, there was a tendency towards the expansion of the Greek banks towards neighbouring countries, including even Ukraine and Egypt, in combination with a decrease in their number via mergers and acquisitions. This tendency has been partly reversed owing to the financial difficulties banks encountered during the economic crisis that burst in 2010. The Greek banks have also been adversely affected by the Private Sector Involvement programme agreed upon in November 2012 that incurred losses, owing to the haircut of the Greek sovereign bonds in their possession. It must be noted, though, that the European Central Bank was exempted from the haircut of the Greek sovereign bonds in its possession, which were purchased at 70% of their nominal value, resulting in Greece having to pay back to the European Central Bank the 100% of their nominal value. Greek banks' liquidity rapidly deteriorated in June 2015 due to massive money withdrawals following a protracted period of political instability and uncertainty about Greece's stay in the Eurozone, resulting in the imposition of capital controls that were fully abolished as of 1 September 2019. Another tendency that accrued recently involves the selling of Greek banks' daughter companies, engaging in activities other than banking. There are currently twenty-two foreign banks operating in Greece, that is twenty branches of banks incorporated in other EU

Member States, operating in Greece under the 'single license' regime as well as two branches of banks incorporated in third countries. The important sector of shipping finance is conducted to a great extent by non-Greek banks operating from time to time via repose.

14. The Bank of Greece, the central bank of the country, which supervises the activities of state-owned and private banks and is responsible for the implementation of the Eurosystem's monetary policy, introduced stricter auditing procedures at the beginning of 1990 and banks are required to report regularly on their affairs. Initially, in 1991, an act was passed for establishing the source of large sums of money in an attempt to reduce money laundering and the effect of the huge black market, which is estimated to form up to 30% of the national economy. In that regard, recently introduced Laws 4734/2020 and 4816/2021 harmonized Greek legislation with the comprehensive EU framework on the prevention of the use of the financial system for money laundering and terrorist financing as well as on combating money laundering by criminal law.

15. As far as insurance companies are concerned, a detailed analysis is offered in Part I below.

16. Investment firms after the booming period of the 1990s have been reduced in numbers and volume since the banks and their daughter companies are the basic intermediaries for investments and further due to the reduction of the demand for investments in the Stock Exchange. In 2021, there were forty-seven investment firms incorporated in Greece as well as several branches of EU investment firms and 'tied agents' engaging in the provision of investment services in the Greek market. Formation of closed and open-ended investment funds is booming. Units and similar products have become common features of the domestic market. Currently, there are fifteen undertakings for collective investment in transferable securities, namely Mutual Funds Companies (Anónymes Etairies Diaxeirisis Amoivéon Kefaléon – AEDAK) that have their registered office in Greece.

The Athens Stock Exchange rocketed during the late 1990s, but during the two first decades of the twenty-first century, the index has suffered great losses. On 1 November 2021, the General Athens Stock Market Indicator was around 908 points. On 1 December 2021, there were 156 companies listed on the Athens Stock Exchange. A second 'Stock Exchange Centre' had been founded in Thessaloniki in 1995, currently renamed 'Hellenic Central Securities Depository', engaging in the provision of central security depository services.

V. Currency Legislation and Monetary Regulation

17. From 2001, the Euro has been introduced in Greece, and the monetary policy is entrusted to the European Central Bank.

18. Greece has liberalized the movement of capital within Europe by Presidential Decree 96/93, which was extended to abolish all restrictions on the movement of capital internationally by Presidential Decree 104/94. As per Directive 2009/110/EU, the source of money intake needs to be justified (anti-money laundering policy).

Greece entered the European Exchange Rate Mechanism in early 1998, devaluing the Drachma by 14% in order to do so, and announcing a wave of privatizations and reforms in order to meet the criteria for entry into the European Monetary Union in 2001.

There is steadily a greater reliance on market factors in determining interest rates, and the Bank of Greece no longer sets the minimum savings deposit and lending rates, nor sets compulsory investment distribution among various forms of investments.

19. The general government debt amounted to 205.6% on top of the Gross Domestic Product at the end of 2020, while at the end of 2019, the corresponding figure was 180.5%. The core inflation rate for 2019 was formed at 0.5% and for 2020 at –0.7%. As known, Greece was since 6 May 2010 under the scrutiny of the IMF, EU and the European Central Bank (ECB), following the stand-by agreement signed. As of March 2010 and up until recently, Greece experienced incapacity to reach the international markets and due to its deficit, as mentioned above, signed a stand-by agreement with the IMF, EU and the ECB. On 14 February 2012, Memorandum of Understanding II was adopted and on 7 November 2012, it was amended, providing for further restructuring measures to be realized by the Greek Government. Finally, on 13 August 2015, Memorandum of Understanding III, encompassing further measures for the stabilization of the Greek economy, was passed on by the Greek Parliament. On 21 August 2018, this last Memorandum's duration expired, and typically the heavy surveillance regime was terminated, albeit Greece's commitments deriving from the aforementioned programme will continue to be in force for decades to come, as the country's public debt remains immense and will be only gradually de-escalated.

VI. Insurance Business: General Organization and Special Features

20. Insurance business in Greece is not highly developed but is showing growth. Premiums correspond to 2.42% of Gross National Income (2019 data). It should be noted that the market share of social insurance is larger than in other EU countries, a fact which affects the percentage of Gross National Income taken up by insurance.

21. In 2019, fifty-four insurance companies were in operation in Greece. The insurance companies operating in Greece managed assets amounting to EUR 19.3 billion, of which EUR 15.9 billion are placed in investments. Direct premiums in the same year amounted to EUR 4.44 million. Of the total direct premiums in 2019, EUR 2.24 million represent non-life premiums, and EUR 2.2 million represent life premiums.

The totality of fifty-four insurance undertakings, which were active in Greece during 2019, comprises:

Life insurance companies	6
Non-life insurance companies	34
Mixed insurance companies	14
Total	54

Table 1 shows the distribution of premiums in the Greek market in 2019, in terms of non-life and life insurance.

Table 1 Distribution of Premiums in the Greek Market in 2019

Non-life Insurance Premium Per Class of Insurance for 2019	*%*
Accidents	2.22
Sickness	12.19
Land vehicles	10.32
Aircraft	0.01
Ships (sea, lake and river vessels)	0.52
Goods in transit	1.05
Fire and natural forces	15.32
Other damages to property	4.04
Motor vehicle liability	38.13
Aircraft civil liability	0.05
Civil liability for ships	0.24
General civil liability	4.35
Credits	1.66
Suretyship	0.10
Miscellaneous financial losses	2.54
Legal expenses	1.65
Assistance	5.60

Life Insurance Premium Per Class of Insurance for 2019	*%*
Life insurance	67.27
Life insurance linked to investment funds	16.87
Permanent health insurance	0.00

Life Insurance Premium Per Class of Insurance for 2019	%
Capital redemption operations	0.00
Management of group pension funds	15.86

Source: Greek Association of Insurance Companies, http://www1.eaee.gr/sites/default/files/annual_stat_report_2019_gr.pdf.

22. As mentioned above, a special feature of the Greek insurance business is that social insurance takes up a major part of insurance normally covered by private insurers. Non-life, non-compulsory consumer insurance is still at a relatively early stage, with a limited number of people insuring their houses. Life insurance has, however, developed considerably over the past years. The classes of life insurance, in particular, coupled with coverage against the risk of hospitalization and management of group pension funds are expected to grow substantially. The so-called second pillar of the pensions' system, encompassing the occupational retirement provision schemes, is still not sufficiently developed in the country, but future development may be expected after the recent transposition of the IORPs II (No. 2016/2341) Directive. A corresponding growth in consumer insurance is generally likely in the near future. Insurance coverage of other kinds concerns mainly commercial and industrial risks.

23. A symptom of the lack of development of insurance undertakings is that the volume of business conducted by intermediaries still remains disproportionally large compared to the amount of business undertaken directly by insurance undertakings. As a result, the commission received by intermediaries is significantly high, while numerous companies and persons are currently active in the insurance intermediary business. As a matter of fact, many consumers, when concluding insurance contracts, quite often rely on the person of the intermediary rather than on the services provided by the insurance company or on its brand name. Therefore, intermediaries commonly perceive that insureds constitute part of their personal clientele instead of the insurance company – a view which is not unjustifiable. There is an ongoing process to reduce the cost of intermediation, which was indeed unreasonably high in Greece. The online sale of insurance products still remains rather confined.

§2. Historical Background of Insurance and Insurance Legislation

24. Long before the appearance of the first Greek insurance company in Greece, insurance companies were established and managed by Greeks in the greatest European commercial centres.

The first Greek insurance company to operate abroad was founded in Trieste, Italy, in 1789 under the name 'Societa Greca d'Assicurazione'. Insurance in Greece first made its appearance for marine risks in the seventeenth century. Insurance during those times was practised by mutual organizations covering hull risks.

25. The first domestic company was established in the newly founded Kingdom of Greece by virtue of King Otto's Royal Decree 1/13 of June 1836 under the name 'Achaean Insurance Company of Marine Transport', seated in Patras, which was also the first company limited by shares which was founded in the modern Greek state. By 1900, sixty-three insurance companies were operating in Greece. This sharp rise in the number of insurance companies coincides with a peak in Greek maritime commerce. However, this steep augmentation of insurance enterprises resulted in the decline of most of them since supply greatly exceeded demand in what was then a very small and quite poor market. It should also be noted that, in 1846, nine insurance companies under Greek names were launched and run by Greeks in Constantinople, possibly before the appearance of the first insurance companies in Greece.

26. The first foreign company was established in Greece in 1839 under the name 'The Adriatic Insurance Company'. It had the exclusive right of writing fire insurance, and Greeks living in Trieste were its major shareholders. After the establishment of the first insurance company, there followed, among other companies, the insurance companies 'Archangelos', 'Agira' and 'Phoenix'. The company 'Essling & Co' which represented the Italian company 'RAS' was granted the exclusive right, by Royal Decree, to write fire insurance in Greece. 'Phoenix', which was the first company established on a basis similar to a contemporary enterprise, went bankrupt thirty-five years after its foundation in 1857, but today the company is again active, being acquired in 2007 by Groupama.

27. There are four periods in insurance enterprise legislation. The first one comprises the period from the liberation of the Greek state until 1917 during which the insurance enterprise operated basically on the same grounds as any other enterprise. From 1917 until 1970, the insurance enterprise was regulated by specific laws. After 1970, new legislation was issued modernizing the operation and supervision of insurance companies, while after 1981, the process of harmonization of insurance undertakings' legal framework to EU law began.

Marine Insurance Law is mainly contained in the Greek Code of Private Maritime Law (CPML) of 1958 which has replaced the relative sections of the Greek Commercial Code (although the precise rendering would be 'The Law on Commerce', it will be hereinafter called 'the Commercial Code'), which, in turn, was based on the Napoleonic Code de Commerce. It should be mentioned that the Insurance Contract Act (ICA – Law 2496/1997), which provides for the provisions governing the general part of all insurance, including marine insurance, has also replaced the relative sections of the Commercial Code.

The main legislation on Insurance Undertakings is Law 4364/2016, which transposed EU Directive 2009/138 on the taking up and pursuit of the business of Insurance and Reinsurance (Solvency II). The aforementioned law replaced the previous legislative framework on insurance enterprises that mainly comprised of Legislative Decree 400/1970 and its numerous amendments that ensured compliance with relevant EU legislation, e.g., the Second and Third Life and Non-life Directives on insurance enterprises. The business activity of intermediaries is governed by Law 4583/2018 that harmonized Greek legislation to Directive 2016/97 on insurance distribution and replaced the pre-existing legal framework, namely Law 1569/1985 (as expanded by Law 2170/1993, which regulated the activities of insurance brokers) and Presidential Decree 190/2006 that had transposed Directive 2002/92 on insurance mediation (IMD).

The legislation relating to the insurance policy itself has been radically overhauled by the introduction of Law 2496/1997 ('the ICA'), which completely replaced the Commercial Code's provisions on insurance policies. It came into force on 17 November 1997. The legislation has taken into account the draft Directive on the insurance contract, which was later on abolished. In many ways, ICA precedes the respective provisions of EU law. It should be noted that ICA's drafters broadened the branches of insurance governed by legislation and introduced a framework which would protect the consumer against unfair terms and conditions while allowing the flexibility which the business user requires in his dealings with insurance companies.

§3. Sources of Insurance Law

I. Legislation

28. Insurance legislation can be divided into two categories: legislation regulating the insurance enterprise and legislation regulating the insurance contract. The insurance enterprise is governed by Law 4364/2016, Legislative Decree 551/1970 on the Insurance of Ships and Aircraft, as amended, and Law 4583/2018 on Insurance Intermediaries and Distribution of Insurance Products. The application of Law 4548/2018 on Incorporations and the general provisions of the Commercial and Civil Codes are applied supplementarily.

29. As mentioned above, the insurance contract is regulated by the provisions of the ICA, and the marine insurance contract is regulated by the CPML of 1958 (Articles 257–288). Special issues of both insurance enterprise and insurance contract are regulated by the Private Aviation Code (PAC) of 1988 and by Law 489/1976 on Compulsory Motor Insurance, as amended. Other relevant laws are, among others, Law 1796/1988 on the Fund for Insurance of Export Credit as codified into Law 3912/2011, Law 3455/2006 on the Supervision of Financial Conglomerates and Law 3877/2010 on the Creation and Operation of the Fund for Agricultural Insurance.

30. Even though the custom is supposed to be equal to written law, being a source of law, it cannot abolish or modify a legislative provision. Business usage plays an important role in insurance law and especially in reinsurance. Business usage, to a large extent, also regulates co-insurance.

II. Governmental Regulations

31. Insurance law is implemented by Laws, Presidential Decrees, Ministerial Decisions and Decisions of the Insurance Supervisor. Presidential Decrees are issued upon the proposal of the Minister of Economy. They regulate particular detailed matters within the scope of the legislative delegation. Ministerial Decisions and Presidential Decrees are issued pursuant to the legislative delegation and are of equal status to the law while they are, among others, used as a means of harmonization of the Greek legislation with EU law. They are treated as enhanced authority and prevail over ordinary law, as their status is constitutionally safeguarded. For instance, the basic amendments of the pre-existent Legislative Decree 400/1970 on Insurance Enterprises were effected by virtue of such Presidential Decrees.

32. The most important Laws, Presidential Decrees and Ministerial Decisions regulating private insurance can be divided into two categories. The first category involves insurance undertakings, intermediaries and supervision, and the second category encompasses insurance contracts (including motor insurance).

The laws relating to the first category are as follows:

(1) Law 4364/2016 on the taking up and pursuit of the business of (re)insurance, harmonizing Greek legislation with EU Directive 2009/138 (Solvency II).
(2) Legislative Decree 551/1970 on Insurance Undertakings covering Marine and Aviation Insurance.
(3) Law 4583/2018 on the Distribution of Insurance Products.
(4) Law 3867/2010 on Guarantee Fund of Life Insurance.
(5) Several Decisions of the Insurance Supervisor, namely Bank of Greece, which are altered on a regular basis.

The laws relating to the second category are as follows:

- Law 2496/1997 (ICA).
- Law 3816/1958 (Code of Private Maritime Law).
- Law 1815/1988 (Code of Private Aviation Law).
- Law 489/1976 on Compulsory Motor Third-Party Liability Insurance (codified law) which has been amended to date several times.

III. Private International Law

33. International insurance law is the part of private international law, determining the law that rules the insurance contract. With the exception of marine and aviation insurance, the applicable law on insurance contracts (and especially on contractual relations) is not regulated by Article 25 of the Greek Civil Code, according to which the applicable law, in principle, is the law agreed and determined by the parties and, in the absence of such agreement, the most appropriate law to the contract, but by Regulation 593/2008 ('Rome I').

34. Rome I provides for the following cases:

(1) In the case of non-life insurance, where the risk is located outside the EU, the parties can freely choose the applicable law (Article 3). If no choice has been made, then applicable law is the law of the place of establishment of the insurer (Article 4). In case the insured is also a consumer, the law of the country of his usual residence must be taken into consideration (Article 6).
(2) In the case of a non-life insurance, where the risk is located within the EU, the parties can choose between: (a) the law of any Member State, where the risk is located at the time of the conclusion of the agreement; (b) the law of the Member State, where the insured has its usual residence; (c) in case of insurance agreements, covering risks, which are restricted to incidents related to a Member State, which is different from that, where the risk is located, applicable is the law of that Member State; (d) when the insured exercises a commercial or entrepreneurial activity or is a freelancer and the insurance agreement covers two or more risks, which concern such activities and are located at different Member States, applicable is the law of any of such Member States or the law of the Member State, where the insured has his usual residence (Article 7). In the case of non-choice, applicable is the law where the risk is located during the conclusion of the agreement (Article 7). In case the insurance concerns large risks, the parties can freely choose the applicable law. If no choice has been made, then applicable law is the law of the Member State, where the insurer has his usual residence (Article 7).
(3) In the case of life insurance, the above restricted right of choice of the applicable law includes the law of the nationality of the Member State of the insured as well (Article 7). If no choice has been made, applicable is the law where the risk is located during the conclusion of the agreement (Article 7).

35. The applicable law cannot override *jus cogens* provisions (e.g., the rule of overinsurance), the mandatory provisions of the law of the forum and upon fulfilment of certain conditions of the law of the country, where the contractual requirements must be fulfilled or have already been fulfilled (Article 9).

IV. Case Law

36. Case law is a secondary source of law in Greece. Although judicial precedent is not binding for the Courts, it constitutes, in fact, a useful aid for the judge while applying the law. Due to the fact that few legislative provisions exist on insurance contract law, the role of case law is more important than in other areas and has formed a significant means of interpretation of the most widely used insurance contract terms, including those of compulsory motor insurance. Insurance supervision is ruled by a more detailed and rather technical legislative framework and case law has not been greatly developed in this field.

§4. Dispute Settlement and Arbitration

37. Disputes between the insurer and the insured, the insurer and the collaborating intermediary or the insured and the intermediary as well as insurance, reinsurance and intermediary companies and their personnel are resolved by ordinary courts. Special procedures are provided for the resolution of labour law disputes, for premium payment disputes and motor accident disputes.

Disputes concerning taxation are resolved by administrative courts. The same applies to administrative sanctions imposed on insurance companies for infringing legislation regarding their supervision. The Council of State, the Supreme Administrative Court in Greece, has exclusive jurisdiction for the resolution of disputes between the state and insurance companies. Such cases concern, for instance, disputes over the Decision of the Insurance Regulator (i.e., the Central Bank of Greece) on the establishment of an insurance company as well as the peremptory or temporary withdrawal of a company's or a branch's operation licence.

Criminal prosecutions are resolved before criminal courts.

38. Trials can be rather long-lasting. The Magistrate's Court is competent for the settlement of disputes the object of which does not surpass EUR 20,000, while jurisdiction of the Single Member Court of First Instance extends to disputes the object of which is up to EUR 250,000. All cases that are not submitted to the jurisdiction of either Magistrate's Court or the Single Member Court of First Instance are submitted to the jurisdiction of Multimember Court of First Instance. The Civil Procedure Code provides for that labour disputes, motor accident disputes and disputes regarding premiums are submitted to the jurisdiction of Single Member Court of First Instance (instead of the Multimember Court of First Instance), even if the value of their object surmounts EUR 250,000.

Most court cases regarding insurance companies concern recovery claims (mainly disputes between insurers and transporters) and motor accidents. These cases can be settled through the procedure of 'security or interim measures', on condition that there is a risk of losing the possibility to collect money in the future because the defendant is suspected of not being solvent after the lapse of the period which the litigation procedure consumes. The decision issued is executable within days or even hours. For instance, in case of a maritime claim whereby the insurer has been subrogated to the insured's rights may request the conservatory seizure of the ship belonging to the third party who damaged the insured. Nevertheless, the insured's entitlement to demand conservatory seizure of the insurer's property is only theoretical, meaning that the Court will not accept such petition because the legal framework on supervision of insurance companies and the superintendence of the Supervisor of Insurance eliminate the element of danger, ensuring that the insurer will always possess available funds for the satisfaction of the insured's claim. In this regard, the insurer's property representing its technical provisions (reserves) can be seized only pursuant to an executable decision requiring the insurer to pay insurance money.

39. Only few of these disputes are resolved by arbitration. These disputes mainly concern recovery claims in marine insurance, where an arbitration clause is usually incorporated in the charter party or the bill of lading. Only in a few cases, the insurer and the insured agree to submit the dispute to arbitration after it has arisen. If the parties or the arbitrators have not reached an agreement about the person of the umpire, the latter is appointed by the Single Member Court of First Instance of the area where the arbitration is about to take place under the agreement. The award of the arbitration tribunal cannot be appealed before ordinary courts as far as the examination and legal assessment of facts is concerned. However, the violation of procedural rules is contestable before the Courts. Reasons for contesting the award are, among others, nullity of the arbitration agreement, issuance of the award after the expiration of the term of the arbitration agreement, appointment of the arbitrators against the law, violation of the principle of equity between the parties, contradictory or vague justification of the award and contradiction of the arbitral award to good morals and public order.

As regards the law applicable to arbitration, the 1958 New York Convention on the recognition of arbitration awards has been ratified by Greece. National law on arbitration is incorporated in the Code of Civil Procedure, Articles 867–903.

40. Expert adjudication was also provided by the previous Law 400/1970. This procedure differed from arbitration: it concerned only the final settlement of the extent of the damage and not the claim in its entirety. Typical fire policies included a standard term on expert adjudication, in order to secure that the dispute would not be submitted to court unless the extent of the damage had been previously established by the expert. The Court was bound to take into consideration the experts' decision. This agreement was regarded by the Supreme Court as arbitration restricted to one specific dimension of the dispute. The agreement was valid only if concluded in writing and signed by both parties. Thus, the standard term of the policy on expert adjudication had fallen into disuse and was applied only exceptionally on condition that the policy had been signed by both parties or that they both accepted the procedure willingly. The latter was not usually the case since insureds, unlike insurers, did not form organized associations and because insureds were prejudiced against the objectivity of the experts' adjudication, given that experts usually cooperate with insurers.

According to Act No. 88/05.04.2016 of the Executive Committee of the Bank of Greece on Complaints-Handling by insurance undertakings, insurance companies must form a mechanism for extrajudicial management and enquiry of complaints of the insureds, policyholders and third persons entitled to the insurance money. According to the relevant provisions, the insurance company should inform the complaining party of the procedure it implements regarding the handling of his claim, provide him a written answer no later than fifty days since the reception of the complaint as well as inform the complaining party that the activation of the complaints-handling mechanism does not interrupt the limitation period of the insured's claims.

§5. CONSUMER PROTECTION

I. General Remarks

41. Consumer protection is regulated by various statutes, which fall under two categories: provisions which deal with consumer protection directly and provisions which deal with the subject indirectly. The first group comprises Law 2251/1994 'on consumer protection'. Although consumer protection is not constitutionally safeguarded, theory and case law acknowledge its significance which originates from the general principle of protecting the weaker party. In order to identify the weaker party, both parties' financial status and the nature of the transaction are taken into account.

42. Law 2251/1994 'on consumer protection' has harmonized the respective EU Directives and deals with manifold aspects of consumer protection, such as unfair business-to-consumer commercial practices, misleading advertising, protection of consumers in respect of distance contracts, distance marketing of financial services and injunctions for the protection of consumers' interests.

43. Law 2251/1994 gives consumer associations the right to bring class actions against producers accused of use of unfair terms or provision of inadequate services to consumers. These associations may apply for court orders declaring that general trading terms must be amended as incompatible with business ethics and consumer protection. The Court can award financial compensation for 'moral damage'. Moral damage awards shall be proportionate to the severity of the allegations and the size of the company/producer. Certain consumer associations have brought actions against several domestic and foreign insurance companies regarding their general terms and conditions, and the Courts have demonstrated willingness to strike out unfair terms as abusive.

II. Consumer Protection and Insurance

44. The ICA introduces provisions which protect the policyholder, the insured and the beneficiary irrespective of whether they can be regarded as 'consumers' according to the meaning ascribed to this term by Law 2251/1994 or not. The consumer is commonly defined as the person who acts outside his trade, business or profession. However, Law 2251/1994 on consumer protection, in its initial form and before its recent amendment (2018), defined consumer (in the context of the application of certain provisions) as the ultimate receiver of goods or services. On the contrary, according to the Greek ICA's mandatory provisions, all policyholders are worth the extra protection, irrespective of whether they fall under the notion of consumer, except for five types of large commercial insurance.

Moreover, in five cases, ICA allows for amendments of the insurance contract's terms to the detriment of the policyholder but only if the latter acts for purposes which fall outside the scope of his trade, business or profession (i.e., if the policyholder is not a consumer). In all other cases, ICA provisions are 'unilaterally compulsory' in the sense that the insurance contract can include amendments to them only if such amendments improve the policyholder's (insured's or beneficiary's) position by extending its rights. Those five cases are as follows:

(1) The law provides that the policyholder is obliged to take all necessary measures to avoid or mitigate the insured loss and to comply with the insurer's instructions. However, it is provided that an agreement to the contrary shall be acceptable if the policyholder or the insured has concluded the insurance contract for purposes relating to its trade, business or profession.
(2) The law provides that the insurer can avoid coverage when the insured event originated from deliberate acts or omissions of the policyholder. Further, the ICA allows the imposition of the same sanction, upon contractual agreement, in cases where the insured event resulted from negligent acts or omissions of the policyholder, given that the latter concluded the insurance contract for purposes which fall outside the scope of its trade, business or profession.
(3) After the occurrence of the insurance event, the policyholder is obliged to safeguard its rights against any third party while he is liable to compensate the insurer for any loss or damages sustained in breach of this obligation, insofar the insurer may be subrogated in such rights. It may, however, be agreed that the insurer shall be discharged of the liability to pay the insurance money if the insured breached his obligation to mitigate his loss/damage, in case the policyholder concludes the insurance for purposes related to its trade, business or profession.
(4) The law provides that if, at the time of conclusion of the insurance contract, the insured property was described only in general terms and concerns items which will only be subject to the insured risk in the future, the policyholder or the insured shall be obliged to specify the insured object as soon as they acquire knowledge thereof concerning the nature of the items and their insured value, as well as any other detail defining the contract, in accordance with the terms and conditions of the policy. Nevertheless, it is provided that if the policyholder or the insured concludes the policy with a view to covering professional risks, the parties may reach an agreement in terms contrary to the above stipulations.
(5) The rule of Article 19 of the ICA on insurance against the risk of fire can be deviated to the detriment of the policyholder in its entirety, in case the latter concludes the contract for purposes related to its trade, business or profession.

Furthermore, in five types of commercial insurance, the ICA allows the parties to agree on deviations from any provision of the ICA. In these five cases, the criterion for the validity of the deviation is not the capacity of the policyholder as a consumer but solely the type of insurance. The relevant commercial insurance are the following: insurance for the carriage of goods, credit insurance, suretyship insurance, maritime and air insurance. The justification of the admissibility of deviations in these five types of insurance lies in the fact that they are concluded by policyholders who act for their trade/business. However, the exclusion's proper interpretation suggests that it does not extend to suretyship or credit insurance concluded in the context of consumer transactions.

45. The law requires that the policy is contained in a written document. The policyholder must receive all contractual terms with the policy document. All general and special terms must be clearly stated. A similar system also applies to the information to be given to the insured, prior to the conclusion of the policy. These rights to information may only be waived by agreement in specified exceptional circumstances.

The insured is entitled to additional protection under the ICA which amended previously standing legislation on pre-contractual disclosure. While under the old law, failure to disclose relevant facts automatically invalidated the contract, the ICA gives the insurer only the right to amend the terms or the premium payable under the contract or the right to terminate the contract on fifteen days' notice for negligent or intentional breach of the disclosure obligation. However, if the policyholder deliberately fails to disclose the required information, the insurer can terminate the contract with immediate effect. The insurer has only one month from discovering the true facts to make his decision. The insurer cannot, though, seek to alter or withdraw from a contract based on his standard questionnaire if circumstances which were not the subject matter of a question have not been disclosed. The insured has a duty to inform the insurer about new facts which might aggravate the risk within fourteen days of becoming aware of them. If it can be established that the insurer would not have concluded the contract or would have concluded it on different terms, had he been aware of such facts, he has one month's time limit to decide whether to amend or terminate the contract. The policyholder may also request a renegotiation of his non-life insurance premium if the risk remits significantly during the term of coverage. If the insurer fails to respond to the premium mitigation request or refuses to make such reduction, the policyholder shall be entitled to terminate the contract.

III. In Particular the Right to Object

46. One of the main novelties of the ICA is the right given to the insured to withdraw from the contract or object to certain terms. The insurer has the duty to inform the policyholder clearly of his multiple rights. The insurer is penalized for failure to do so in various ways.

In all personal insurance contracts, as well as all property policies of over one year's duration, the insured has the right to withdraw from the contract without justification within fourteen days from delivery of the policy or from the moment he was informed by the insurer of such right. If the insured is not notified of the aforementioned fluency, his right to withdraw shall lapse two months after the first premium's payment.

In the event that the contents of the insurance policy differ from the contents of the application for insurance, such inconsistencies shall be deemed to have been approved from the commencement of the contract, provided that the policyholder does not object in writing thereto within one month following the receipt of the insurance policy and that the insurer has duly informed the policyholder of such inconsistencies, as well as of the policyholder's right to object. Information should be tendered by the insurer in writing or through a relevant notice on the first page of the insurance policy written in such a way as to make the notice readily distinguishable from the other parts of the document, thus enabling it to be easily noted by the reader. The insurer must also supply the policyholder with a separately printed specimen of the notice of objection. If the insurer fails to inform the policyholder of his rights or to equip him with the above-mentioned specimen notice, the inconsistencies shall not be binding for the policyholder, and the contract shall be deemed to have been agreed in accordance with the contents of the application.

As noted above, the insured must be equipped with a copy of the policy and all its general and special terms and conditions. The information includes what is required to be provided to the applicant before the conclusion of the insurance contract (i.e., applicable law, procedure and time of settlement of the policyholder's written requests, address of the headquarters or the branch or the agency editing the insurance policy, etc.). The information to be provided differs in life and non-life insurance. In addition, further information concerning the insurance policy must be offered after the harmonization of Greek law with the Solvency II Directive.

If the insurer fails to supply the policyholder with any of the above information or to convey the insurance terms and conditions, the contract shall be deemed to have been concluded on the basis of the policy. In that regard, such contract is governed by all the insurance terms and conditions and the additional information, if any, which determine the individual contract, provided that the policyholder does not object in writing within fourteen days of the policy being delivered. Should the aforesaid time limit expire without any action being taken, the contract shall be deemed to have come into effect from the date on which it was concluded. The aforesaid time limit shall not commence if the insurer fails to inform the policyholder of his right to object to the contract and in the absence of the aforesaid information. The insurer must notify the policyholder of the above right in writing or by an easily legible notice appearing on the first page of the policy and supply the policyholder with a separately printed specimen of the notice of objection. The policyholder's right to object shall expire after the lapse of ten months from the date on which the first premium was paid. If the policyholder raises an objection, the contract shall be avoided. The burden of proving that the appropriate documents were delivered lies with the insurer. These provisions are 'strict' law and are not open to alteration against the interests of the insured by agreement between the parties.

47. The insured is further assisted in claiming under the policy owing to the extension of the notification period from three days, under the previous legislation, to eight days from discovering the occurrence of the insured loss, under the ICA. Breach of this requirement does not invalidate the policy, as was the case under the previous legislation, but allows the insurer to claim damages for any additional costs incurred by the delay. The limitation period for claims arising out of property insurance has been extended from three to four years, and the respective limitation period for life contracts has been extended from three to five years.

48. According to legislation on the supervision of insurance undertakings (Law 4364/2016, Article 152 para. 3), the insurer is obliged to inform the policyholder during the term of the insurance contract about any changes concerning the trade name, legal type and address of the main offices or of the branch or agency, which has acted for the conclusion of the contract. Moreover, the insurer is obliged to inform the policyholder about any changes concerning the list of information which has been provided to the applicant during the pre-contractual stage in life insurance. The insurer is further obliged to inform the policyholder in relation to the latter's possible participation in profits or the outperformance of the technical reserves.

§6. COMPULSORY INSURANCE

I. General Remarks

49. Compulsory insurance, introduced by mandatory law provisions, can be divided into liability insurance and non-liability insurance. Liability insurance is the most common kind of compulsory insurance and includes forty distinguished kinds, out of which the most widespread is the Motor Vehicle Third-Party Liability Insurance (MTPL). The MTPL which covers the relationship between the insurer and the policyholder is the only compulsory insurance governed by several special rules. Most of the compulsory liability insurance provide for the right of direct action of the injured third party against the insurer. Notably, no compulsory personal insurance exist in Greece.

II. MTPL Insurance

50. MTPL insurance is fully harmonized with the EU Directives. Due to detailed regulation, as well as the lack of application of Alternative Dispute Resolution (ADR) systems, i.e., processes that act as a means for disagreeing parties to come to an agreement short of litigation, for car accidents, MTPL has been growing as an important branch of private insurance law.

A characteristic of this branch, introduced for the protection of third parties, is that the injured party can bring a direct action (action dirécte) against the insurer and enjoys greater protection than the insured. As a result, the insurer is also liable in cases where he/she would not be liable towards the insured who failed, for example, to adhere to certain contractual conditions. However, new amendments of Greek MTPL restrict the ability of the insurer who paid indemnity to the injured third party to recover such amount from the policyholder who was in breach of its contractual obligation to maintain an effective insurance policy, in only three cases.

III. Other Kinds of Compulsory Insurance

51. Other kinds of compulsory liability insurance include civil liability insurance for oil pollution of the sea, international carrier's liability insurance for damage to goods transported by land, air carrier's liability insurance for damages to passengers and goods, builders' design and construction liability, as well as tour operators' civil liability. Notably, apart from certain kinds of professional liability, still a great number of self-employed professions are not compulsorily insured. As regards the liability of employers for labour accidents, no compulsory insurance exists because no liability exists, provided they have paid their contributions to the Social Insurance Fund. Compulsory insurance is not separately regulated like motor liability insurance, but there are common insurance types which are obligatory pursuant to legislative provisions. Another provision which refers expressly to these forms of insurance is the provision which introduces the direct action for the injured party against the insurer, as well as the provision which excludes (in some kinds of compulsory liability insurance) the possibility of the insurer raising an objection against the third party, regarding its liability based on the contract (e.g., breach of pre-contractual, disclosure obligation, non-payment of premium instalment). Action dirécte is dictated by the need to protect the injured party. This protection would be restricted in the absence of action dirécte since Greek law (Civil Code), contrary to French Law (Code Civil), cannot lead via interpretation to the establishment of a direct action of the injured party against its insurer. Article 26 of the Greek ICA sets a general provision for all types of compulsory liability insurance, which can be summarized in two basic principles: first, the third party has a right of direct action against the insurer, and second, breaches of the insurance policy's terms by the insured cannot justify refusal of compensation to the third party. However, the above principles are not realized in most cases of compulsory liability insurance. Article 26 paragraph 5 of the ICA provides for that a decision of the Minister of Development and the competent Minister in each case, published in the Government Gazette, shall specify the following: the authorities or corporations authorized to receive insurers' notices, the procedure to be followed to certify compliance with the requirements of compulsory insurance, as well as the necessary details pertaining to the operation of compulsory third-party insurance. It is also provided for that these provisions of Article 26 shall not apply if the competent department or legal entity has not been specified. It must be noted that to date, the above-mentioned decision has not been issued.

52. The most prevalent category of non-liability compulsory insurance was the own damage insurance of sea passengers. This kind of insurance was operated by the 'Seamen's Pension Fund' by affixing a stamp on tickets for sea travel in place of a premium. It functioned as a sum insurance because a lump sum was paid to the passenger upon injury. The protection offered to passengers did not limit the liability of the responsible party.

Nevertheless, doubts had been raised as to the compliance of the operation of this kind of insurance with EU requirements. Since 2011, this insurance has been abolished insofar (EU) Regulation 392/2009 on the 'liability of carriers of passengers by sea in the event of accidents' has extended the scope of application of sea carriers' liability for damages to passengers to coastal shipping (i.e., carriage between ports of the same country), ensuring passengers' adequate protection.

53. There have often been shaped-up proposals by Draft Committees for the extension of compulsory insurance to other branches, both liability and non-liability, such as those relating to compulsory insurance for the owner of buildings against earthquakes as well as against other catastrophic risks. Nevertheless, until today, such proposals have not led to the establishment of relevant compulsory insurance.

Part I. The Insurance Company

Chapter 1. The Insurance Company: Its Form

§1. Mutual Insurance and Premium Insurance

I. Mutual Insurance

54. Even though mutual insurance goes a long way back in Greece, it plays a minor role in the local insurance market. Law 945/1979 on the Accession of Greece to the EC provided that mutual insurance could not be practised for life but only for general insurance. However, mutual insurance companies are entitled to conduct life insurance business in Greece provided that they are established in another EU Member State and operate in Greece through a branch or under 'freedom to provide services' (FoS). It is noted that the EU Directive 2009/138 (Solvency II) which, *inter alia,* encompasses provisions on the establishment of insurance undertakings provides that foreign insurance undertakings are free to operate in another EU Member State in the same form as in their home country. There is, therefore, no restriction in Greece regarding the form of mutual insurance provided that it legally operates as such in its home country.

Mutual insurance are active in Greece, in particular in the field of coverage of job-related risks for members of the same profession.

The above-mentioned prohibition contained in the Act of Accession of Greece to the EU and repeated in Law 4364/2016 on the taking up and pursuit of insurance does not, however, prevent Greek public law undertakings from conducting mutual life insurance business.

There is no mutual life insurance company currently operating with its seat in Greece, nor was there any before Accession.

Mutual insurance are widespread within Greek maritime interests (P&I, war risk, etc.), but the mutual insurer is almost always a non-Greek entity, i.e., entities registered in home countries, such as UK, Sweden, Norway, Cyprus, Bahamas. In 2007, a new type of Maritime Mutual Insurance was introduced to cover maritime claims, hull, goods transport, as well as P&I.

55. The rules governing mutual insurance do not differ from those governing premium insurance. In both cases, a policy is issued, and both are ruled by insurance contract law. Moreover, consumer protection granted to consumers insured by way of mutual insurance is equal to the protection tendered to other insured consumers.

56. The mutual insurance company may operate under four forms:

(1) As a mutual insurance cooperative for non-life insurance which must be joined by at least fifteen founders.
(2) Under any form recognized by the law of an insurance enterprise operating in any EU Member State.
(3) Maritime Mutual Insurance.
(4) As a public law enterprise, the form of which has not yet been determined as none has operated so far.

57. Mutual insurance companies are, in practice, divided into 'large' and 'small' companies. 'Large' mutual insurance companies are governed by the rules applying to all insurance companies, including those relating to matters such as technical provision, scheme of operations, preservation of funds covering the minimum capital requirement, etc.

'Small' mutual companies, instead, are exempted from the application of some of the provisions on insurance supervision which apply to insurance undertakings. Nevertheless, the aforesaid exemption of mutual companies is dependent on the fulfilment of two criteria which are not directly related to such cooperatives' seize: (a) the mutual insurance company in question must conclude only non-life insurance; and (b) it must have reinsured the entirety of its business to another mutual insurance company. The reasoning for 'small' mutual companies' exemption from the application of the supervisory legal framework applicable to common insurance companies and large mutual companies lies with the proportionality principle, since conformity with all the obligations imposed on large insurance undertakings would, in practice, preclude small mutual insurance companies from accessing the market.

Maritime Mutual Insurance do not fall under the above categories of mutual insurance. The structure of this type of mutual insurance is tailor-made for operating mutual insurance, while the structure of the other type of mutual insurance is based on the existing form for common cooperatives.

II. Premium Insurance

58. Greek insurance business is conducted mainly through premium insurance, which operates only under the form of a joint-stock company. Insurance undertakings have the form of a specially regulated joint-stock company limited by shares (SA – société anonyme), which is permitted to conduct exclusively insurance business. However, insurance business does not consist exclusively of underwriting policies but encompasses other insurance services as well, such as those offered by insurance intermediaries.

59. Until recently, marine insurance could be written by Lloyd's of London which was entitled to operate in Greece through representative offices of Lloyd's brokers. This long-standing exception provided in favour of Lloyd's of London has been abolished since the implementation of Law 4364/2016. Thus, after Brexit, any insurance with Lloyd's can be written in Greece only through Lloyd's insurance undertaking established in Belgium which has passported its activities in Greece, operating under freedom to provide services (FoS). Insurance may also constitute the exclusive business of a public law insurance undertaking or a foreign insurance undertaking established in Greece under the form of an agency or branch office, or especially for European Economic Area (EEA)-based companies under the EU freedom of services regime.

The form of the foreign insurance undertaking established in Greece is immaterial; i.e., the undertaking may take whatever company form is accepted in its country of seat in order to exercise insurance business, provided the seat is situated within the EU, regardless of whether this company form is also provided by Greek law for Greek insurance undertakings. If the company's seat lies outside the EU, the only form acceptable is that of an SA. However, under certain prerequisites, an undertaking whose seat lies outside the EU may be granted certain business advantages for its business in Greece, provided that the same company is already established in another EU Member State.

60. The corporate form for the operation of premium insurance companies is necessary, owing primarily to the fact that such companies provide additional guarantees as they are required to always possess a minimum share capital. However, insurance undertakings' solvency is not secured by the rather inadequate minimum share capital provided for common SAs (EUR 25,000) but mainly through other means imposed by the special legislation applicable to them, concerning their solvency guarantees [Minimum Capital Requirement, Solvency Capital Requirement – *see* below, paragraphs 71 et seq.].

61. There are no insurance companies operating under a form other than that of the mutual or premium insurance company. Although certain services provided by non-insurance companies are similar to insurance money, they are not identical. For instance, pension supplements, lump sum payments in case of death, and technical services may all be undertaken by undertakings irrespective of their form as companies or partnerships. If, however, such services are considered to constitute provision of insurance money, then they can be performed only by insurance companies.

Furthermore, there is a particular type of insurance enterprise called the 'Seamen's Pension Fund', which is a public law corporation that carries out social insurance. However, this Fund was also active in compulsory bodily injury insurance for coastal vessel passengers who were obliged to pay the premium along with the fare, as mentioned above (under paragraph 51). In the latter case, this Fund operated as a private insurer. Nevertheless, this function has been abolished as of 2011.

§2. The Public and Private Nature of the Insurance Company

62. Although the law does not prevent public law corporations from writing insurance, the entirety of insurance business in Greece is conducted by private companies. However, an important market share, principally of non-life business, was held by insurance undertakings owned by banks, which in the past used to be controlled by the state.

§3. Factual Data

63. As mentioned above, fifty-four insurance companies were operating in Greece as of 2019. Apart from these, there are also several mutual insurance cooperative funds (e.g., bus-owners' and various local funds) which are of minor importance in the market. On the taxation of insurance companies, *see* Part IX.

Chapter 2. Access to Business

§1. Greek Insurance Undertakings

64. There are certain differences among the prerequisites for the establishment of insurance undertakings, depending on whether they are established in Greece, within the EU or outside it.

The same procedure for obtaining a licence applies to a company wishing to extend its business to other insurance branches.

65. The provisions regarding the prerequisites and the procedure for obtaining the operation licence are harmonized with EU law. The applicant company, whether Greek or foreign, must file its Statute and scheme of operations with the Bank of Greece, which is the Regulator of private insurance, as well as proof that it possesses the required funds covering the applicable Minimum Capital Requirement as well as the Solvency Capital Requirement. Hence, the Bank of Greece supervises, among others, the Statutes' compliance with the provisions on insurance undertakings and joint-stock companies.

The scheme of operations specifies, in particular, the risks the company intends to cover, its guiding reinsurance and retrocession principles, estimates on the costs of setting up and the financial means employed for such costs coverage, as well as a forecast of income and of the operating costs for the first three fiscal years. It also includes a detailed forecast of the financial resources intended to cover technical provisions, the Minimum Capital Requirement and the Solvency Capital Requirement.

66. The novel legal framework on insurance undertakings, i.e., Law 4364/2016, abolished the special provisions on the minimum share capital of insurance undertakings. Nevertheless, Greek insurance companies are obliged to preserve minimum capital requirements, which vary among insurance classes, ranging from EUR 2,500,000 to EUR 7,400,000. These minimum capital requirements were introduced to ensure compliance with the relevant provisions of the Solvency II Directive and equate to the superseded guarantee funds of the previous law on insurance undertakings. Under the latter, these two amounts (minimum share capital and guarantee fund) were equal when the company began to operate, while after the company's activities commenced, the obligation to maintain a guarantee fund increased in proportion to the obligations and responsibilities undertaken by the company.

If it is proved that the undertaking possesses the requested minimum capital requirements and all the prerequisites for the incorporation of the insurance company have been met, namely if the notarial deed pursuant to which the company was established, as well as its Statute and scheme of operations have been submitted, then the Supervisor of Insurance (Bank of Greece) issues the operation licence and approves the Statutes in a single act.

It is to be noted that the Greek Regulator (the Bank of Greece) in June 2012 had published a draft law, amending radically the legal framework of insurance undertakings' operation and supervision, ensuring its harmonization with the Solvency II Directive, which was enacted in 2014. The aforementioned draft law was the basis of Law 4364/2016 which transposed the Solvency II Directive and repealed the pre-existing legal framework on insurance undertakings. Law 4364/2016 provides, among others, some additional prerequisites for the undertaking seeking a licence to conduct insurance and reinsurance business in the country.

§2. Non-Greek Insurance Undertakings

67. Non-Greek insurance companies can be distinguished according to whether they are established within or outside EEA territory. The prerequisite for obtaining an operating licence in Greece is the appointment of a 'legal representative' in Greece, who is either an individual or legal entity. If the legal representative is a legal entity, it must appoint an individual as its representative.

68. Furthermore, every EU insurance company must be furnished with a solvency certificate issued by the Supervisor of Insurance of its home country and a certificate listing the insurance branches through which the company operates in Greece.

69. Non-EU companies must comply with additional requirements, i.e., their minimum capital requirements must be at least equal to those required for Greek companies (i.e., they must possess eligible funds covering the Minimum Capital Requirement and Solvency Capital Requirement), their assets in Greece must equate to one-half of the minimum capital requirement requested for insurance undertakings and one-quarter thereof must be deposited in Greece as a guarantee while they must also have established a branch in Greece. The company must exhibit a satisfactory degree of organization, management and accountancy, and the reciprocity principle must be observed between Greece and the home country.

The solvency margin required for non-EU insurance companies which operate through agencies or branches in one or more other EU Member States may be calculated in relation to the volume of their entire business within the Community by agreement of the Bank of Greece, issued pursuant to an agreement with the supervisory authorities of the other Member States. On certain occasions, the Supervisor of Insurance may release them entirely from the obligation to deposit a guarantee in Greece insofar they have deposited such guarantee in another Member State.

70. Lloyd's of London underwriters used to be a special case in Greek insurance law. Although Lloyd's of London underwriters did not operate via a legal entity, Greek legislation treated them as such (a legal entity) as far as insurance supervision was concerned. The previous legislation on insurance supervision (L.D. 400/1970) explicitly provided that Lloyd's of London could be established in Greece through a general representative. On the contrary, standing legislation on supervision of insurance undertakings (Law 4364/2016) does not provide for the assimilation of Lloyd's of London with insurance companies.

71. As stated above (under paragraph 59), according to a long-standing exception, marine insurance could be written by a Lloyd's underwriter even without the cooperation of the general representative, provided that the policies/cover notes were signed by a Lloyd's broker established in Greece through a representative. The general regulations on common brokers also applied to Lloyds brokers' representatives, who were, therefore, required to obtain professional liability insurance of at least EUR 1,924,560 for a year. Nevertheless, this special regime has been repealed so that, nowadays, insurance with Lloyd's can be written in Greece only through Lloyd's insurance undertaking established in Belgium which has passported its activities in Greece, operating under freedom to provide services (FoS).

Chapter 3. Supervision

§1. Solvency Control

72. State Supervision on insurance undertakings has restrictive effects on the entrepreneur's freedom. These restrictions comply with constitutional provisions and arise from the necessity to protect the insured's interests, which is the basic objective of the legislation on insurance supervision.

The provisions on insurance supervision can be classified according to their purpose. There are provisions which aim at the uninterrupted solvency of insurance undertakings and, generally, at the insured's protection. Such provisions can be characterized as the law of insurance supervision in the narrow sense. The remaining provisions regulating the operation of the insurance enterprise may be characterized as the law on insurance supervision in the broad sense.

73. Solvency control is effectuated by preserving the minimum capital requirement, as well as through technical reserves, insurance investment and the share capital. The issues relating to technical reserves will be further analysed below. The maintenance of the solvency margin is an obligation for all insurance companies, apart from the maintenance of the technical reserves for the coverage of unforeseen or extraordinary events. Thus, the reserve for pending risks (reserve for outstanding claims), which is calculated on the basis of risk-occurrence possibilities, may prove inadequate if the insurance enterprise happens to suffer an unexpected series of losses. It also serves as a reserve for reinsurers' insolvency or long-term adverse financial circumstances. The minimum capital requirement comprises the unblocked assets of the company, the volume of which must grow obligatorily in proportion to the growth of the volume of work.

74. The minimum capital requirement that insurance undertakings must possess is differentiated, in accordance with the insurance services accorded by them. In this respect, the law (Article 102, paragraph 1, lit d of Law 4364/2016) specifies that the minimum capital requirement preserved has to, at least, amount to:

(i) EUR 2.5 million for undertakings providing non-life insurance;
(ii) EUR 3.7 million for undertakings providing life insurance and insurance against liabilities originating from motor vehicles, aircraft and vessels as well as credit and suretyship insurance (classes ten to fifteen);
(iii) EUR 3.6 million for reinsurance undertakings;
(iv) EUR 6.2 million for undertakings providing both life and non-life insurance.

75. As far as the preservation of the requested technical provisions and the minimum capital requirement is concerned, the following observations are noteworthy:

(a) The pledge of assets allocated in insurance investments to cover unearned premiums and outstanding claims provisions is not permitted under the Solvency II Directive (Article 134 paragraph 2). In that regard, the pledge of assets for the establishment of technical provisions is not permissible, even though the relevant Article 106 of Law 4364/2016 on insurance undertakings does not explicitly state so.

(b) Should the minimum capital requirement preserved by the insurance undertaking fall short of the minimum amount required under Article 102 paragraph 2, the undertaking must inform the Bank of Greece in that regard and submit a realistic recovery plan aiming at the restoration of a sound financial position for approval. In case of exceptional circumstances, if the Bank of Greece is of the opinion that the financial condition of the insurance undertaking will deteriorate further, it may restrict or forbid the free disposal of the whole or part of the assets of the insurance undertaking, pursuant to Article 109 paragraph 5 of Law 4563/2016 in order to secure the interest of the insureds.

(c) If the minimum capital requirement is not complied with by the insurance undertaking and the finance scheme submitted is manifestly inadequate or the undertaking concerned fails to comply with the approved scheme within three months from the observation of non-compliance with the Minimum Capital Requirement, the Bank of Greece compulsorily withdraws the authorization granted to the (re)insurance undertaking (Article 114 paragraph 1 lit c).

76. The minimum capital is calculated as a linear function of a set or subset of the following variables: the undertaking's technical provisions, written premiums, capital at risk, deferred tax and administrative expenses. The method for calculating the minimum capital requirement is described in detail by law.

77. The Bank of Greece carries out annual controls of the undertakings' financial situation in order to ascertain their compliance with the provisions concerning the preservation of the minimum capital requirement and publishes the relevant statistical data in its webpage.

§2. Supervision of Tariffs

78. In Greece, there are no restrictions on premium tariffs. The full liberalization of tariffs was realized in 1996. Also, no restrictions exist as to the commissions of the insurance intermediaries.

§3. Supervision of Insurance Conditions

I. General Remarks

79. Since the implementation of the deregulation in Greece in the 1990s, all provisions requiring the compulsory submission of policy terms to the Regulator for prior approval have been abolished. The Regulator, however, retains the right to examine individual cases and demand amendments, if there has been a serious breach of rules, which protect consumers and/or the general good.

II. Motor Third-Party Compulsory Liability Insurance

80. Compulsory third-party motor insurance is governed by the Codified Law 489/1976. The law does not state the terms of the insurance policy itself, but rather sets out the obligations which the insurer has *ex lege* in favour of the third-party claimant, which arise automatically, irrespective of any special terms of the insurer's contract with the insured driver. It must be underlined that the insurer cannot raise defences arising from the insurance policy against the injured third party. Moreover, albeit the terms of the policy itself may vary, the law contains three cases (driving without licence, driving under the influence of alcohol or drugs and use of the vehicle different from the one specified in the policy and the vehicle's registration) where the losses incurred are always excluded from coverage. However, the injured third party has always a claim against the insurer, irrespective of whether the damage falls under one of the above-mentioned permitted exceptions. Consequently, the only difference is that in case the realization of the risk falls within these three exceptions, the insurer can turn against the insured and claim a part of the indemnity paid to the injured party. Thus, although these terms cannot be adduced to the detriment of the injured third party, they may give rise to the insurer's right to claim compensation from the insured driver (in the context of recovery proceedings) for damages paid as a result of the insured's breach of the policy, such as driving while drunk.

Chapter 4. Insurance Investment and Technical Reserves

§1. Insurance Investment

81. Until the harmonization of the Greek law with the Solvency II Directive, a distinction between 'insurance investment in the narrow sense', implying the restricted disposal of insurance companies' assets located in Greece or elsewhere in the EEA intended for safeguarding the interests of the insureds, and 'insurance investment in the broader sense', connoting the unrestricted exploitation of insurance companies' assets which did not function obligatorily as protection for the insureds ('free reserves'), was made. After the introduction of Law 4364/2016, this distinction is not valid since the same principles apply to the investment of the whole portfolio of an insurance company.

82. The assets possessed by (re)insurance companies must be invested according to the prudent person principle (Article 104 of Law 4364/2016). The latter requires that (re)insurance undertakings, regard being had to their whole portfolio of assets, shall only invest in assets and instruments whose risks can be properly identified, measured, controlled and appropriately taken into account by the undertaking, in the assessment of its overall solvency needs. Thus, all assets, in particular, those covering the minimum capital requirement, shall be invested in such a manner as to ensure the security, quality, liquidity and profitability of the portfolio as a whole. In addition, the localization of those assets shall be such as to ensure their availability. However, Law 4364/2016, in contrast to the previous law, neither requests (re)insurance undertakings to invest in specific categories of assets nor subjects their investment decisions to any kind of prior approval or systematic notification requirements.

§2. Technical Reserves

83. (Re)insurance companies are obliged to maintain technical reserves, which have been rebranded as 'technical provisions' as from the application of the Solvency II Directive, regarding all of their obligations towards policyholders and beneficiaries of (re)insurance contracts.

The value of such technical provisions shall correspond to the current amount (re)insurance undertakings would have to pay if they were to transfer their obligations immediately to another undertaking. They must be calculated in a prudent, reliable and objective manner, and their value shall be equal to the sum of the best estimate and a risk margin, over the provisions/reserves concerned. When calculating technical provisions, (re)insurance undertakings shall also take account of: (a) all expenses that will be incurred in servicing their obligations, (b) inflation, as well as (c) all payments to policyholders and beneficiaries, including future discretionary bonuses.

Upon request from the Regulator, (re)insurance undertakings shall demonstrate the appropriateness of the level of their technical provisions, as well as the applicability and relevance of the methods applied, and the adequacy of the underlying statistical data used.

Chapter 5. Accounts

84. Like other incorporated companies, (re)insurance companies are subject to statutory audits of their accounting documents. Prior to the introduction of special legislation on that issue, insurance companies were obliged to conform to the general provisions of the pre-existing Codified Law on Societés Anonymes, which referred to accounts. Harmonization of Greek law to the provisions of the first set of EU Directives on accounts and their amendments was effectuated between 1986 and 1994. The aforementioned Directives were amended by the recent Directives 2013/34 and 2006/43 (both referring to accounts), which were transposed to the Greek legal order through the introduction of Law 4449/2017. Pursuant to the provisions of the latter, accounts must be drafted in such a manner that secures transparency and the proper continuity of the company, providing an accurate description of its financial situation, its activities and the formation of reserves.

85. Regard being had to comparative law reasons, it must be noted that until 1984, insurance undertakings applied the same accounting system applied by all incorporations, as there were no separate regulations for insurance companies. Later on, the Special Uniform Accounting Plan for insurance companies was brought into force. Greek insurance companies, as well as branches or agencies of foreign insurance companies established in Greece, were obliged to proceed with the implementation of the Plan by 1985, and so were insurance cooperatives and insurance intermediaries by 1986. Failure to comply with the above time limits resulted in the imposition of fines. The aforementioned provisions have been repealed and replaced, recently.

86. According to the most recent Directive 2013/34 on the annual and consolidated financial statements of certain types of undertakings, the financial statements of public interest entities, medium sized and large undertakings are audited by one or more approved statutory auditors or audit firms. Besides, (re)insurance undertakings are always considered to be public interest entities, irrespective of their size.

Furthermore, in light of the auditors' independence, it is provided that: (a) the key audit partner responsible for carrying out statutory audit rotates from the audit engagement within a maximum period of seven years from the date of appointment and is allowed to participate in the audit of the (re)insurance undertaking again after a period of at least two years; (b) the statutory auditor or the key audit partner who carries out a statutory audit shall not be allowed to take up a key management position in the (re)insurance undertaking before a period of at least two years has elapsed since he/she resigned as a statutory auditor or key audit partner from the audit engagement.

87. The auditors of a (re)insurance company are required to report promptly to the Supervisory Authority, any fact or decision concerning that undertaking of which they have become aware while carrying out the auditing task and which is liable to bring about any of the following:

(a) a material breach of the laws, regulations or administrative provisions which lay down the conditions governing authorization or which specifically govern pursuit of the activities of (re)insurance undertakings;
(b) the impairment of the continuous functioning of the (re)insurance undertaking;
(c) a refusal to certify the accounts or to the expression of reservations;
(d) non-compliance with the Solvency Capital Requirement or the Minimum Capital Requirement.

88. Insurance companies must be audited by approved auditors, licensed by the Hellenic Accounting and Auditing Standards Oversight Board. The latter grants licence for the conduction of audits only to persons who fulfil certain criteria; i.e., they are of good repute, they comply with standardized educational qualifications, they have succeeded in the test aiming to ensure their professional competence, they have completed the necessary three years' practical training, etc.

89. An annual transparency report of the (re)insurance undertaking's auditor is published on the latter's website, within three months of the end of each financial year, which verifies the compliance of the auditor with the quality and procedural standards introduced by EU law.

Part II. The Insurance Contract in General

Chapter 1. General Remarks

§1. Insurance Contracts and Other Contracts

90. Private insurance coverage presupposes a valid contract. This is not required in social insurance. Contracting parties' relationships in social insurance are formed in a dissimilar manner than in private insurance law (for the formulation and function of parties' relations in social insurance, *see* below paragraphs 300 et seq.). General rules of the Civil Code applying to the basic common contracts, such as rules on error, fraud, simulated declaration and declaration made under duress, also apply to insurance contracts.

Coverage by private insurance is thus considered by the Greek legal system as a private affair, governed by the principle of the individual's right to self-determination. The public dimension of private insurance coverage becomes evident, though, in the strictness of legislative supervision. This supervision also affects the insurance contract since it can result in state intervention in favour of the insured, especially when the latter bears the capacity of a consumer.

91. The insurance contract is regulated by the Greek ICA (Law No. 2496/1997). Supplementarily, the Greek Civil Code's chapter on the law of obligations is applied insofar the insurance contract falls, in particular, within the category of continuous obligations. The concept of an insurance contract is defined by mandatory law so that contracts which do not fulfil the relevant legal prerequisites do not qualify as insurance contracts. There is no insurance when there is no insurance contract. Self-insurance does not, therefore, qualify as insurance. The insurance contract is strictly bilateral and, as a rule, no gratis insurance can be concluded.

Furthermore, according to Greek law, an insurance contract is considered as a 'standard form' contract, and in this respect, it is interpreted according to principles which differ from those generally applicable to contracts. It has a commercial character because insurance is always regarded as a commercial activity for the insurer and often in the case of non-consumer insurance, for the insured as well. The contract's commercial character affects matters of both substantive and procedural laws.

§2. Interpretation of the Insurance Contract

92. The insurance contract, notwithstanding its nature as a standard form contract, is governed by the general rules on contracts and is thus interpreted according to both good faith principles (bona fide) and business usage. When it comes to the standard general terms and conditions, interpretation follows the general rule of favouring the insured, and in case of doubt, interpretation is against the insurer who issued the policy. This rule is applied irrespective of the contract's character as consumer or non-consumer.

In cases involving consumer insurance contracts, interpretation follows the EU Directive 93/13 on unfair terms in consumer contracts and Greek Law 2251/1994 on consumer protection, which grant, to some extent, further rights to the insured.

The insurer's allegations brought forward in defence against a claim of the insured are treated like ordinary claims. The fact that the insurer is, in the last analysis, managing other peoples' money and thus engaged in activities that represent broader interests cannot be taken into consideration by the judge in favour of the insurer when resolving the dispute.

§3. Insurance Classes

93. Insurance is classified according to two different criteria. Depending on the way in which insurance cover is provided, the distinction is made between indemnity or non-life insurance and sum insurance. Depending on the risks covered, insurance is divided into indemnity insurance and insurance of persons. Under indemnity insurance contracts, insurance money is based on the extent of the loss. Sum insurance contracts provide for payment of a fixed sum, independently of the existence or extent of the loss. Insurance of persons includes life insurance which is always sum insurance and is distinguished between purely risk-based and risk-based in combination with saving/investment. It includes further health and illness insurance, which can be concluded as either indemnity insurance or sum insurance.

94. Under the chapter 'indemnity insurance', the ICA distinguishes among fire insurance, agricultural products insurance, pollution, transport of goods, credit and guarantee, business interruption and civil liability (compulsory and non-compulsory). These distinctions partly coincide with those between certain insurance classes provided by the legislation on insurance enterprises.

95. Depending on the risks covered, distinctions can be made between: (a) indemnity insurance (property and liability) and insurance of persons and (b) marine and non-marine insurance.

The first pair does not exactly coincide with the indemnity and sum insurance pair since the insurance of persons can also be written as indemnity insurance. As mentioned above, indemnity insurance covers risks associated with the insured's property (either assets or liabilities). Insurance of person covers risks associated with the insured's life (death, survival, accident, health). The second distinction between non-marine and marine insurance owes its existence to historical reasons: the provisions of the original first commercial code regulated marine commerce and, therefore, marine insurance. The regulation of non-marine commerce came about at a later stage and was followed by non-marine insurance law. Even later, with the introduction of the new CPML, the country acquired new marine insurance law which constitutes the basis for marine insurance contracts.

Insurance contract related to marine insurance is the aviation insurance contract.

96. Another distinction is made between property and liability insurance (sometimes referred to in legal literature as 'active' and 'passive' insurance). In property insurance, the loss refers to an object forming part of the insured's assets, e.g., property, claims, anticipated profit, etc. In liability insurance, the loss consists in an increase of the insured's liabilities or the establishment of liability, e.g., debts, obligations, etc. Liability insurance contracts have been regulated for the first time by the ICA.

Further distinctions are made between facultative and obligatory insurance, as well as premium and mutual insurance.

Chapter 2. Insurable Risks

§1. Insurable Risks in General

97. Every risk which can cause damage to a person or property and is thus capable of reducing assets and increasing liabilities is insurable under an insurance contract. There is no differentiation depending on whether the risk refers to movable or immovable goods or on whether the objects are in transit, etc.

98. Risk is the most fundamental element in private insurance. Under the ICA, the policyholder is released from his obligation to pay the premium if, at the time of conclusion of the insurance contract, the insurer is aware of the absence of risk. If, on the other hand, at the time of conclusion of the contract the policyholder (or the insured or beneficiary) is aware of the occurrence of the insured risk, the insurer is released from his obligation to pay the insurance money under the policy and if the insurer was unaware that the risk had occurred, he is entitled to the premiums as well. The principle which governs insurable risks is, in the field of non-marine insurance, that of the 'specificity of the risk'. Coverage is not granted indiscriminately for all risks but only for risks expressly defined in the contract. The specificity of the insurable risk is the main rule of insurance contract law, and the ICA defines the nature of the risk for many types of insurance, its provisions being applicable in the absence of an agreement to the contrary.

99. In marine insurance, 'all-risks' coverage is the rule (*see* paragraph 180). However, through the numerous exceptions set by marine policies, the effect of 'all-risks' principle is reduced. Notably, according to Greek theory, 'all-risks' rule is not the distinguishing feature of marine insurance but of transport insurance.

100. Distinctions among the various kinds of risk are also made by premium tariffs, but their significance lies in the calculation of the premium. The contractual obligation of the insurer to cover the risk agreed on is not essentially affected by the extent of the risks which are determined by the premium tariffs of the specific contract. Reinsurance does not include classification in the sense of first insurance. The industry follows several kinds of reinsurance contracts which apply worldwide.

§2. Restrictions on Insurable Risks

101. Under Greek insurance law, the insurer is free as to the choice of the risk he wishes to cover, provided that he has a licence to conduct the insurance class, corresponding to such risk. Of course, the insurer cannot conclude an insurance contract, which is against the public order. Exceptions from coverage are included in Article 13 Paragraphs 1–2 of the ICA and concern losses incurred due to acts of war, civil war, rebellion and civil commotion. Particularly in property insurance, no cover is provided for losses arising from the natural deterioration of the items insured. The insurer, though, is free to agree to cover the above-mentioned exceptions. Further exceptions may be agreed, provided that they are dictated by the technical requirements of the insurer.

102. The insurer does not normally grant unlimited liability coverage, but he is free to do it. Coverage of civil liability attributed to fraud or intention, coverage whereby the policyholder/insured has no insurable interest on the insured object, as well as coverage whereby both the insurer and the insured know that the risk which has already occurred is null and void, even if the insurer does not want to take advantage of such voidness.

103. The term 'insurable interest', according to Greek law, means the applicant's legal interest in avoiding the loss. In property insurance, Greek theory distinguishes between insurable interest in a broad sense and insurable interest in a narrow sense: insurable interest in a broad sense presupposes that the applicant shall have an interest in the mere non-occurrence of the insured risk, while the insurable interest in a narrow sense requires that the policyholder suffers because of the occurrence of the risk damage equating to the insurance money he claims.

Chapter 3. Formation of the Insurance Contract

§1. General Remarks

104. Private insurance is based on the insurance contract. The ICA requires that the contract is concluded in writing and signed by the insurer. As well as the specific rules set out in the ICA, the general Civil Code's provisions will also be applied. Thus, the insurance contract is valid only if the parties reach agreement on the elements constituting the contract as these are defined by the respective specific provisions of insurance contract law. The insurance contract shall specify at least the particulars of the contracting parties and the name of the person entitled to the insurance money, should that person not be the policyholder. It should also contain: the time span of cover, the subject matter of the insurance and the risks covered ('insured risks'), any limit of the insurer's liability ('insured sum'), any exceptions to cover, the premium and the applicable law, if not Greek.

105. Incorrect declaration of intention by either party, such as a declaration made in error, a declaration of intention which was not taken seriously but was only fictitious or based on a mistaken intention, is regulated according to the Civil Code. However, the relevant articles of the Civil Code are only of theoretical value in insurance law, as the formation of an insurance contract requires an application by the insured and a written contract, so that a claim based on incorrect declaration has not been reported to date.

106. Before concluding the insurance contract, the applicant can sign an application form prepared by the insurer containing printed terms which are to govern the insurance contract.

§2. Issuing the Insurance Policy

107. The ICA requires the insurer to issue a policy and a cover note where appropriate. The policy, however, is the only evidence of the agreement. The contract is valid, even if no document is issued. Further, the obligation to issue a policy is provided by fiscal law provisions which consider the policy as a payment receipt. Failure to issue the policy may give rise to sanctions by the Tax Authority. Such sanctions may only be imposed if the insurer has accepted to provide coverage and not in the case where he denies having agreed with the applicant for insurance, i.e., if he has not issued a policy because he believes that no agreement has taken place.

The signature of the insurer or his representative is sufficient and is reproduced mechanically or electronically. There is no need for the policyholder to sign the policy in order for the latter to be valid as a document of proof.

§3. Proof of the Insurance Contract

108. The policy form is required ad probationem and not ad solemnitatem. However, the law requires the insurance contract to be proved by the policy and not by witnesses. The existence of the contract may be proved through witnesses only if the parties prove that the issued policy has been accidentally lost. The ICA confirms the long-held view that the issue of the policy is an obligation of every insurer who has concluded an insurance contract by an express term.

§4. Transfer of the Policy

109. The policy is not negotiable *ex lege*. The insurance relations cannot be transferred through a transfer of the policy, with the exception of marine transport (cargo) insurance (*see* paragraph 210). However, the law allows the conclusion of the non-life insurance by negotiable instrument (negotiable policy). In this case, the clause 'to order' must be mentioned in the policy. The insurance relations may then be transferred by endorsing the policy. Insurance policies may also be issued to the bearer.

§5. Interim Insurance Contract

110. Interim insurance is concluded with the issue of a cover note, which allows for immediate coverage before the actual policy is issued. Cover notes are governed by the ICA, which states that they must contain the basic information required for the policy, as well as the date and place of their issue. Interim coverage is common in fire and marine insurance when the parties do not have knowledge of all essential elements required for the issue of the actual policy.

The interim insurance contract confers the parties all the rights and obligations of an ordinary insurance contract for a short period of time. Interim contracts are interpreted by taking into consideration the fact that the insurer has undertaken coverage for risks whose details he was not aware of, expecting to obtain such knowledge of details by the end of the term for which the interim cover note has been issued.

§6. Other Requirements for the Validity of a Contract

111. An important requirement for a valid non-life insurance contract is the existence of a legitimate interest of the insured party in preventing the occurrence of the insured risk that is of an insurable interest in a broad sense (*see* above, paragraph 103). The absence of any legal interest renders the insurance contract void. Another prerequisite is the insurer's capacity as a licenced insurance company. The requirements for the validity of every contract of obligation according to general law, such as the capacity of the parties to enter into juridical acts in binding form, apply as well. This capacity depends, among other things, on the age and state of mind of the persons involved.

112. However, the absence of the above-mentioned requirements is not necessarily assimilated to a contract which has never taken place. If the necessary legal requirements for the operation of the insurance enterprise are not met through the insurer's fault (as, for instance, in cases of licence withdrawal), it is not considered fair for the insured to bear the consequences of the insurer's conduct and the contract still creates obligations for the 'pseudo insurer'.

Chapter 4. Obligations of the Insured

§1. Payment of the Premium

113. The main obligation of the insured is the payment of the premium. In case of breach of this obligation, the insurer can cancel the contract and demand payment by filing a lawsuit against the insured. Under Article 6 of the ICA, coverage is provided only on payment of the entire premium or the first instalment, unless there has been an agreement otherwise. In case of non-payment of a successive instalment, the insurer may terminate the contract one month after the service of a written notice informing the insured that the contract will be terminated if the policyholder continues not paying the delayed premium.

114. The insurer can set off his claim for the premium with the insurance money owed. The payment of the premium must be effected in cash. Since the insured's performance consists of payment in cash, it must be executed under the general law, and thus payment at the place of the insurer's residence is required. In practice, however, it is usually the insurer who collects the premium.

§2. Obligations upon Conclusion of the Contract

115. When concluding the insurance contract, the policyholder must provide information or circumstances of which he is aware and which are objectively material for the assessment of the risk and must also answer every relevant question posed by the insurer. If the insurer issues and presents to the applicant a standard questionnaire, usually including a petition formula, the insured cannot be held liable later on for failure to disclose information not requested in the form, or for failure to fill in certain sections of the questionnaire, cover being provided in any case. If for any reason beyond the control of the insurer or the policyholder, information or circumstances objectively essential for the assessment of the risk were not made known to the insurer, the latter is entitled to terminate the contract or request its variation. The insurer has one month from the date on which he becomes aware of the information or circumstances to decide whether to exercise this right. If the insured negligently fails to comply with the duty of disclosure, the insurer is also entitled to these rights. If the insured risk occurs prior to the variation or termination of the contract taking effect, the insurance money is reduced in proportion to the difference between the premium set in comparison to the premium which would have been demanded if the failure to disclose had not taken place. If the failure to disclose was fraudulent, the insurer is entitled to terminate the contract, within the same one-month time limit. If the insured risk occurs during this time limit, the insurer is released from the obligation to pay the claim. It should be noted that the provisions on non-negligent and negligent failure to comply with the duty to disclose do not apply to life and sickness insurance.

§3. Obligations During Term of Coverage

116. During the period of coverage, the insured is required to inform the insurer of any incidents or circumstances which might have significantly aggravated the risk and which therefore might have affected the insurer's decision to issue the policy on the given terms. Notice to the insurer must be tendered within fourteen days from the insured's acquisition of knowledge of the relevant facts. The insurer then has the right to terminate the policy or alter its terms. There is a similar configuration as to the above-mentioned non-disclosure of material circumstances of the risk.

117. Under the ICA, if the insured risk reduces significantly, the policyholder may require a proportionate reduction of the premium. If the insurer refuses or fails to respond within a month from the request, the policyholder may terminate the policy. This right does not apply to changes in the insured's health in relation to life or health policies. If the policy was issued while the insured or the beneficiary of the insurance money was aware that the risk had been already realized, not only the insurer is not liable to pay the claim but also he is entitled to all premiums up to the end of the policy term.

§4. Obligations upon Occurrence of the Loss

118. As soon as the loss occurs, the insured is obliged to inform the insurer within a maximum of eight days (ICA, Article 7.1) and take all necessary measures to avoid or mitigate the loss. The standard of care is that of an ordinary uninsured in similar circumstances. Failure to notify the insurer within the time specified cannot lead to avoidance of the contract but entitles the insurer to seek compensation for any loss suffered thereof. If reasonable attempts are made to mitigate the loss, the insurer is bound to reinstate the insured's expenses, even if such expenses exceed the insured sum. The parties can conclude an agreement to the contrary only in case the contract is concluded for business purposes. If the insurance money covers only a part of the loss, the insurer will be obliged to refund only a proportional part of the expenses, unless the expenses were incurred following solely the insurer's instructions.

Failure to mitigate would give rise to the policyholder's liability in damages to the insurer under general law. Furthermore, the insured has an obligation to follow the insurer's instructions. Violation of this obligation brings about the same consequences.

Chapter 5. Obligations of the Insurer

§1. General Obligations

119. The insurer is bound to provide coverage during the whole period of his contractual obligation. If the loss occurs, the insurer must pay the insurance money without delay as soon as the cause and extent of the damage are determined and the surveyor's report is submitted. In case of delay, the insurer is liable to pay default interest. More specifically, the insurer is obliged to pay default interest: (a) once a court action has been commenced, (b) if a fully particularized letter before action has been served on the insurer or (c) if the insured is a merchant and the insurance was concluded for business purpose, in which case default interest is owed from the date of the occurrence of the loss. On 30 November 2021, the default interest stands at 7.25%. The rate is fixed by the law and adjusted from time to time to account for inflation. In the latter case (c), the interest is calculated, according to case law, from the day of the accident or, according to a different view, from the date when it became possible to estimate the extent of the damage.

120. Greek law and practice accept only exceptionally bad faith damages against the insurer because the default interest absorbs the financial damage of the insured. Only in the case that a very heavy breach of good faith has been reported and the relevant claim is accepted, the insured is entitled default interest, in addition to insurance money.

121. If the parties are in dispute over the extent of the insurance money due, the insurer has no right to refuse all payments until the settlement of all the disputed aspects. Article 7.7 of the ICA requires insurers to pay any undisputed sums at once until the assessment of the loss' full extent.

122. The insured is not entitled to bring an action against the insurer in order to force him to be capable of paying the insurance money at any time, that is to oblige him to possess adequate funds to this end. Only the Supervisory Authority is competent to force the insurer to perform his solvency obligations. The insured can report the insurer to the Regulator if there is evidence that the insurer is in breach of its solvency obligations.

§2. Particular Obligations of the Non-life Insurer

I. General Remarks

123. The provisions on subrogation, overinsurance and multiple insurance apply in non-life insurance. Non-life insurance is governed by the principle of avoidance of the insured's enrichment. Provisions regarding subrogation, overinsurance and multiple insurance do not apply to life insurance contracts. Only personal accident and illness insurance can be concluded either as indemnity insurance or as sum insurance.

Private insurance is thus divided into two categories: indemnity insurance and sum insurance. Each of these is regulated by different principles, hence the 'dualism' of insurance contract law.

II. Underinsurance

124. In active insurance, where coverage concerns the entire value of the insured interest (full coverage), the sum insured is equal to the actual value of the subject matter of insurance at the time of occurrence of the loss. In cases where the sum insured is lower than the actual value at the time of occurrence of the loss, the insurer's obligation is reduced proportionately and the insured is burdened with part of the damage. This rule is known as the 'proportion rule' of underinsurance. It is immaterial whether the sum insured was equal to the actual value of the insured interest upon conclusion of the contract and the reduction in value took place later, during the period of coverage.

Thus, the proportion of the actual value of the insured interest to the insured sum is equal to the proportion of the damage to the payable insurance money. If, for example, the insured sum is half the actual value of the insured interest, the insurance money will accordingly amount to one-half of the loss.

125. Deviation from the underinsurance rule by way of contractual agreement is valid since the rule is not mandatory. This can occur in the case of a policy containing the clauses 'new for old' or 'first loss', usually applied in industrial risks and entailing payment of an additional premium, or in case the insurance contract contains a stipulation as to the insured object's agreed value. The agreed value may be shaped as open to automatic revision, in which case a 'new for old' clause is combined with an agreed value provision. The initial assessment of the insured object's value can be also agreed as automatically renewable, based on a specified index (e.g., the Commodities Exchange).

In order to determine whether underinsurance exists, the value of the insured interest at the time of the loss must be taken into account, instead of its value at the beginning of coverage.

It may be concluded from the above that the underinsurance rule reflects the proportionality between contracting parties' obligations and not the indemnity character of non-life insurance.

III. Overinsurance

126. If the sum insured is higher than the actual value of the insured interest at the time of occurrence of the loss (overinsurance), the insurer is not liable for the amount exceeding the actual value of the insured interest. The overinsurance rule is the counter-rule to underinsurance. Overinsurance derives from the indemnity character of non-life insurance, and it does not, like underinsurance, express exclusively the proportionality between the service and the consideration of the insurer and the insured, respectively.

The insurer must return the premium corresponding to the amount exceeding the actual value of the insured interest unless the insured has fraudulently concluded overinsurance, in which case the contract is void, but the insurer acting in good faith may retain the premium earned. The fraudulent conduct exists, according to case law, when the insured knew that the value declared was much higher than the actual one.

127. The existence of overinsurance is ascertained, as with underinsurance, by taking into consideration the actual value of the insured interest at the time of the loss and not at the time when the contract was concluded.

If a contract on agreed value has been concluded, the insurer is bound by the agreed value, irrespective of what the actual value of the insured interest will be at the time of loss, provided that the agreed value corresponds to the value which the insured interest was expected to have during the course of the policy.

128. The Supreme Court of Cassation has ruled that overinsurance is prohibited for reasons of public order. Even if the insurer has no objection to overinsurance, such an agreement is not valid. In other words, it is not left to the contracting parties to decide on overinsurance, and if they do so, any person having a legal interest may challenge the validity of the contract. A deviation from the rule is accepted only for an agreed value contract. Considering that public order is disrupted when insurance's function as indemnity is violated owing to overinsurance, slight overinsurance is allowed provided there is a reason for it and the insurance's indemnity character is preserved. Agreed value contracts which lead to overinsurance are valid as, in this case, overinsurance operates as an instrument facilitating loss' assessment.

IV. Subrogation

129. Subrogation is another expression of the indemnity character of non-life insurance. Thus, in the case where both the insurer and a third party are obliged to compensate the insured for the accident, the latter cannot be satisfied cumulatively. The insured's rights against the third party are automatically transferred to the insurer (legal cession) up to the amount of the insurance money received by the insured. The insured preserves his claim for indemnity towards the third party but only for the amount of his loss that was not covered by the insurance money. If the insured is satisfied by the third party in the first place, his claim for collection of insurance money is reduced accordingly.

130. Since subrogation entails an *ex lege* and not a contractual assignment of rights, no stamp duty is owed. It is noted that normally the assignment of claims is subject to a stamp duty of 2.4%, which is imposed in addition to the stamp duty payable on the indemnity received. In practice, insurance policies mention that all the insured's claims regarding indemnity against any third party will be assigned to the insurer, even though this clause is occupied by the provision mentioned above.

However, such a clause becomes necessary in some cases where foreign law is applicable or in cases where the contract is not valid as an insurance contract.

131. Subrogation places the insurer in the judicial position held previously by the insured regarding his right to claim damages based on the civil liability of the third party responsible for the damage. Thus, the insurer is the successor of the insured regarding that particular claim. According to the prevailing view, subrogation transfers not only the insured's substantive rights but also his procedural rights. For instance, procedural rights are those deriving from procedural contracts, governing the procedure for the obtaining of evidence or the choice of jurisdiction: a typical procedural right is the one deriving from a contract's arbitration clause, as is usually the case with bills of lading. Thus, if the carrier has caused damage to the insured property, and the insured has a claim against him based on a bill of lading containing an arbitration clause, the insurer, after paying the indemnity, is bound by this arbitration clause and cannot invoke, in his defence, the absence of such a clause in the policy. The same would apply if the contract contained a clause stipulating foreign law and practice as applicable or if it contained a foreign jurisdiction clause. As for substantive law, the part of prescription already lapsed by the time of subrogation as regards the insured is considered to have accrued also for the insurer who subrogates the former in his claims. The insurer cannot claim that the remaining period is too short for the exercise of his claim. However, the ICA states that if the insurer is subrogated to the claim of the policyholder, the claims of the latter against the third party shall not be subject to prescription before the lapse of six months from the date of subrogation, provided that the subrogation took place before the prescription or the expiry of such claims.

132. The provision which places the insurer in exactly the same judicial position as the insured before subrogation (Article 14 ICA) is aligned with the Civil Code's principle according to which contracts concluded to the prejudice of a third party are invalid. If, following subrogation, the insurer enjoyed a broader substantive or procedural right than the insured, there would be a deterioration of the judicial position of the debtor vis-à-vis the insurer which would be regarded as unacceptable under the general law.

One occasion in which prescription is interrupted under Greek law is the lawsuit's filing. If only a part of the sum is paid, and subrogation refers solely to this part, the prescription is interrupted only for this part of the claim. For the remainder, even if the claim is unified, limitation period continues to run. It is further disputed whether the insurer is permitted to file a lawsuit in his own name against the debtor before paying the insurance money. Article 14.1 of the ICA states that the insurer is subrogated to the claims to the extent of the indemnity paid. The insurer may lodge and serve the lawsuit but only if insurance money is paid before the Court hearing. Otherwise, the lawsuit shall be rejected as premature. The insurer may not file a lawsuit in the insured's name since Greek law provides no possibility for filing a lawsuit in another's name. Thus, in cases where the law provides a short limitation period for the debtor, as in the case of a claim against the domestic carrier of goods by land for inability to provide or late delivery or damage to the goods where the claim is time-barred in six months, the insured is obliged to consummate the proceedings for the valuation of the loss' extent rapidly so as not to lose his right to recovery. This matter has concerned insurance practices since it has often proved difficult to obtain a full valuation of the loss before prescription accrues. The ICA grants additional protection to the insurer, by providing that the insurer has a six-month period following the subrogation in which he can validly bring an action against the third party, even if the remaining limitation period to which the insured himself was subject was less than six months. It is, of course, possible for the insured himself to file the lawsuit in time, in which case, after payment of the insurance money, the insurer continues the trial in his name without any legal complications. The question of whether the insured is contractually obliged to file the lawsuit himself to preserve the insurer's claim from prescription is resolved on a case-by-case basis. Courts have often expressed the view that the insured does not lose his right to claim insurance money from the insurer due to his failure to file the lawsuit in time because the insurer should have paid the insurance money within this period. This case law does not rule out the possibility of holding the insured liable if the insurer's delay in paying the insurance money was justified due to the nature of the damage: in this case, the insured breaches his obligation, under insurance contract law, to safeguard the insurer's rights. As a sanction, the insured will be obliged to pay compensation for damages to the insurer, the amount of which is not necessarily equal to the value of the claim lost. Article 14.3 of the ICA expressly stipulates that the policyholder, insured and beneficiary have an obligation to safeguard their rights against the third party. Failure to comply with this obligation results in liability to compensate the insurer's losses incurred thereby. The insurer is not subrogated to the rights of the policyholder if the latter's claims are brought against the insured or the beneficiary, their ascendants, descendants or persons dwelling with the insured or beneficiary or the insured's representatives, unless such persons are liable for acting with intent.

133. The *ex lege* transfer of the insured's rights to the insurer requires the previous payment of the insurance money. Special legislation on the Greek Social Insurance Institution, that is the National Organization for Healthcare Services (EOPYY) which has substituted its predecessor, 'Social Insurance Institution', introduces an exception to the aforesaid subrogation rule as regards the rights of persons insured by EOPYY towards damaging parties: according to this provision, such rights are automatically transferred to EOPYY from the time they arise, irrespective of the time that the insureds collected the indemnity. Therefore, the private motor liability insurer is not released from his liability if he compensated the injured third party in case that the latter was insured by EOPYY. The Social Insurance Institution may claim the same amount again from the insurer precisely because the latter has not paid the person entitled to such payment. The insurer, before paying the injured third party, demands confirmation that the latter is not covered by EOPYY or an indication of the extent of social insurance, in which case the insurer pays the surplus amount.

134. The subrogation of the insurer to the insured's rights means that the insurer's judicial position cannot ameliorate or deteriorate in relation to the judicial position of the insured. As subrogation is enacted by way of assignment of rights *ex lege* and not by virtue of the contract, the contract's invalidation cannot affect subrogation. In practice, the payment receipt includes a clause on an assignment which reinforces the insurer's judicial position before the third party because, even if the insurer's *ex lege* right to subrogation is successfully contested by the third party, the insurer's contractual right to subrogation remains unimpaired. The insurer's right is successfully contested when the third party proves that no indemnity was paid or that there was no insurance contract. However, according to Greek law, the third party cannot invoke objections arising from the insurance contract, such as that the insurer should not have proceeded to payment because the insured had failed to fulfil certain contractual obligations.

V. Multiple Insurance

135. When the insured property has been insured against the same risk more than once by the same or different insurers, at the same or at different times, there is double or multiple insurance, as applicable. Under the ICA, if the insured concludes subsequent insurance(s) over the same risk, he is obliged to notify the previous insurer of the new contract(s) and of the insured sum(s). Multiple insurance contracts are valid up to the total value of the insured loss, but in no case beyond that sum. Unless the contrary is agreed, multiple insurers are jointly and severally liable up to the insured sum stipulated in their policies. The insurer can also insert a clause pronouncing that, if he is not notified of subsequent policies, his liability is limited to the extent of the loss not covered by the first policy. Fraudulent failure on the part of the insured to notify the conclusion of other insurance allows the insurer to cancel the policy.

Co-insurance combined with overinsurance is the case where the policies have been concluded simultaneously.

§3. Particular Obligations of the Life Insurer

136. Life insurance covers an unspecified 'need' which is estimated by the contracting parties with the help of subjective criteria. Therefore, the rules of overinsurance, double, multiple and successive insurance as well as the provision on subrogation do not apply to this type of insurance. Further, courts do not apply these rules in cases of personal accident and illness insurance, which have been concluded as sum insurance. Courts have ruled that the insured can receive full indemnity for the expenses arising from the occurrence of a personal accident not only from the insurer but also from the liable third party since 'human health is priceless'. Courts have also held that in personal accident policies, the clause which assigns the insured's claims against the third party to the insurer is not valid. However, this principle does not govern social insurance where legal cession is provided for the social insurer, as mentioned above (paragraph 132).

Under the ICA, there is, however, a special provision which states that accident and illness insurance concluded under the indemnity system are subject to the subrogation rule. It is important to mention that, according to Greek law, in accident and illness insurance, the principle of prohibition of enrichment is not applied even if such insurance are concluded as indemnity insurance, unless otherwise provided by the policy.

Chapter 6. Insurance and Third Parties

§1. Liability Insurance

137. The ICA introduced special provisions on third-party liability insurance as well as special provisions on compulsory third-party liability insurance. Third parties cannot bring a direct action against the liability insurer (i.e., of the insured party), except for the cases of compulsory third-party liability insurance, including the compulsory MTPL insurance which is regulated by the Codified Law 489/1976. In Greek legal theory, it is not disputed that non-compulsory liability insurance concerns exclusively the interest of the insured and not the interest of the injured third party, so that in non-compulsory liability insurance, no right of direct action against the insurer can be granted based on substantive law. However, from procedural law's viewpoint, the claimant third party is entitled to file a 'third-party lawsuit' or 'derivative action' against the insurer in order to force him pay the insurance money to the insured so that this money is directly attributed to the claimant. The idea behind the derivative action is to enable a creditor exercise his debtor's rights if the latter refrains from pursuing his rights against his debtors.

138. A derivative lawsuit is in line with the contractual relationship of the parties, in the sense that the third party cannot acquire more rights against the insurer than the insured has. In compulsory MTPL insurance, though, the injured third party can raise claims against the insurer even if the latter is not obliged to provide coverage to the insured, for instance, in case the latter has breached some important terms and conditions of the policy.

§2. Non-liability Insurance

139. All types of insurance can be concluded under the form of 'insurance for the benefit of a third party' or 'insurance for whom it may concern'. In these cases, a triangular liability relationship is established between the insurer, the insured and the policyholder.

The policyholder in insurance for the benefit of the third party does not act as the insured's agent. He acts in his own name but on behalf of a third person who is the insured. The policyholder is personally responsible vis-à-vis the insurer regarding the fulfilment of the obligations arising out of the insurance contract. Furthermore, it is possible for the insured to preserve his right of submitting direct claims against the insurer, his rights being independent of the policyholder's approval unless a different contractual structure is provided in the policy.

However, it is possible that the person concluding the policy was, in fact, acting as agent of the insured and not as policyholder of insurance for the benefit of a third party. In this case, the agent acts in the name and on behalf of the insured. In the latter case, if the agent concludes an insurance contract with the insurer, i.e., he is the contracting party, he acts in the name and on behalf of the insured who is directly bound by the insurance contract.

140. It should be noted that life insurance against the death of a third person, who is called 'the person of the risk', is not regarded as insurance for the benefit of a third party as the latter is regulated by the ICA. However, insurance for the benefit of a third party is possible to be stipulated in life insurance, as it is the case with non-life insurance. Life insurance for the benefit of a third party exists in case the policyholder remains the person at risk but provides a third party as the beneficiary of insurance money payable upon the occurrence of the insured event (death or survival of the person at risk) or upon policyholder's request for the repurchase of the policy. Even though the beneficiary in life insurance is the equivalent of the person for the benefit of whom the policyholder concludes a contract, the policyholder is not assimilated to the insured in non-life insurance because the beneficiary in non-life insurance has only rights and no obligations, as it is the case with the insured in the non-life insurance concluded for the benefit of a third party.

Sum insurance is considered as insurance for the benefit of a third party when the person whose health is exposed to the risk of accident or illness and is the beneficiary of the insurance money is other than the policyholder. A relevant example is an enterprise which concludes life and accident insurance for its personnel (group insurance): the members of the enterprise's personnel whose life and health are exposed to the risk are the beneficiaries of the insurance money, while the enterprise is the policyholder.

141. If the capacities of the policyholder and of the insured coincide, then the policyholder is also the beneficiary of the insurance money. This is the case with non-life insurance. In sum insurance, though, the beneficiary of the insurance money is not always the insured. For instance, in life insurance of a third person's life (not insurance for the benefit of a third party), the beneficiary is also the policyholder since the latter and not the third party (whose life has been insured) can sustain financial loss after the materialization of the risk, unless the policyholder has designated a third person as beneficiary: as mentioned, in life insurance a third person can be stipulated as beneficiary, such person not necessarily being neither the person at risk nor the policyholder. It is self-evident that, in life insurance against the risk of death, if the beneficiary has not been designated by the policyholder, the persons entitled to insurance money after the death of the person at risk are his heirs.

142. If the beneficiary is not the same person as the policyholder, the beneficiary can bring an action demanding payment of the insurance money. Nevertheless, the policyholder is also entitled to file a lawsuit against the insurer claiming payment of the insurance money to the beneficiary. If the policyholder in life insurance against the risk, e.g., of survival, claimed payment of the insurance money to himself instead of the beneficiary, the lawsuit would be rejected and its filing would not interrupt prescription unless the policyholder had reserved the right to withdraw the beneficiary.

143. Fire policies sometimes contain a standard clause, known as a 'bank clause', formulated by Professional Bodies of Insurers. Bank clauses refer only to banks and other credit institutions. In the latter case, the third beneficiary bank is neither the policyholder nor the insured but a simple loss payee. If a borrower has taken out a bank credit secured with a mortgage or pledge on his movable or immovable property, the bank requests him to insure the property in question by a fire insurance contract if there is not already such coverage (the bank may request coverage against other risks as well), and further requires that a 'bank clause' is included in the fire policy of such property. By virtue of this clause, the bank obtains the right of a direct claim against the insurer which is independent of any eventual objection arising from the contract and brought forward by the insurer against the insured (such as the insured's failure to pay the premium or violation of his pre-contractual obligations).

§3. Assignment of the Insurance

I. Contractual Assignment

144. There are two ways of assigning the insurance claim: contractual and *ex lege* assignment. A contractual assignment can take place before or after the loss occurs. The insured assigns either a future claim for an amount as yet undefined or a specific claim after the loss occurs. In neither case does a transfer of the contractual relationship take place. A transfer of the 'contractual relations' would take place if the person insured were to change, and upon the insurer's agreement. The insurer's agreement to a contractual assignment is not necessary in cargo marine insurance, as mentioned below (paragraph 210), as well as in cases of sale or transfer of the insured object, when provided by law or contract. As to the transfer of the 'contractual relations' in compulsory liability insurance, *see* paragraphs 253–254.

145. After the claim is assigned, the assignee is not substituted in the position of the insured/assignor. The latter continues to bear all obligations under the insurance contract.

The assignment becomes effective when the relevant contract has been concluded and notified to the insurer. No particular legal form is required. After the conclusion of the contract of assignment, the insured is not entitled to turn against the insurer, even if the notification of the contract's conclusion to the insurer has not yet been made and in spite of the fact that the Civil Code requires the contract of assignment to be notified to the debtor.

The contract of assignment can be proved by a relevant note on the policy to that effect. The omission of such note does not render the assignment contract void unless the policy provides so or if the policy has been issued as a negotiable instrument, in which case all changes in insurance relations are valid only when noted on the policy.

II. Ex Lege Assignment

146. If an asset insured under indemnity insurance is encumbered with a mortgage or pledge, the right to raise a claim against the insurer is transferred *ex lege* to the mortgagee or the pledgee, who become the only parties entitled to lodge such claim, regardless of whether the amount secured is lower than the insurance money. Only after the creditors secured with the above rights have received the indemnity may the insured collect the remainder, if existent.

Chapter 7. Termination of the Insurance Contract

§1. General Remarks

147. Except for specific deviations, the insurance contract terminates: (a) upon expiration of the fixed term for which it has been concluded; (b) upon termination of the contract due to a delay in the payment of premium instalments; (c) upon termination of the contract due to the alteration or aggravation of the circumstances of the risk; (d) if the insurable interest has ceased to exist; (e) upon expiration of the risk; (f) if the insured object is in any way alienated (sold, donated, etc.); (g) if the policy is terminated by virtue of a special clause conferring such right of termination; (h) upon termination due to succession regarding the contractual relation; (i) in life insurance, when the insured has exercised his right to surrender the insurance; (j) if the policy provides further reasons for the termination of the insurance contract.

§2. Termination upon Breach of the Insured's Obligations

148. As regards termination in the particular case where the insured violates his obligation to pay the premium, the ICA provides that the insurer has the right to terminate the insurance contract by written notice tendered to the policyholder, stating that further delay in payment of the premium shall entail the contract's termination. Termination becomes effective after a lapse of one month from the date of tendering of the relevant written notice to the policyholder.

149. As regards the termination of MTPL insurance, the law provides that no cancellation is effective vis-à-vis the injured third party unless the insurer has given a sixteen-day notice of cancellation to the insured via registered mail. In other forms of compulsory liability insurance, the termination or suspension of the insurance cover cannot be invoked against the injured third party before the lapse of one month from the date the insurer notified such termination or suspension to the Authority or legal entity designated for this purpose.

Part III. Property and Liability Insurance

Chapter 1. Fire Insurance

§1. Particular Obligations of the Fire Insurer

150. Fire insurance is the oldest branch of non-marine insurance. It covers damages caused by fire, thunder and, in the absence of an agreement to the contrary, explosion and other related risks, even if not resulting in a fire. Additionally, unless the contrary is agreed, fire insurance covers theft and other losses incurred during the course of the insured event or immediately thereafter, as well as those arising from emergency measures taken to ascertain, avert or limit the damage caused. In this last respect, fire insurance covers indirect losses caused during the insured's attempt to reduce the extent of the main loss. The insured's obligations under a fire insurance contract are the same as those provided in the general part of the ICA. The most important of these are the following.

151. The insurer is released from the obligation to cover damages if the fire was the result of fraudulent behaviour or of the insured's reckless actions carried out with the knowledge that damages could most probably occur, as well as if it can be attributed to gross negligence or intentional act of the policyholder, those dwelling with him, representing him, or those entrusted professionally to safeguard the insured item. Thus, fire insurance also covers cases where the loss has occurred due to slight negligence of the insured. The fire insurer may, however, lawfully restrict his liability by inserting a clause in the policy excluding coverage in the case of insured's slight negligence, but such restriction would not be valid in the case of consumer policies. Finally, insurance cover is not provided if the fire is attributable to war, civil war, rebellion or civil commotion, except for terrorist actions of individuals or groups. Nevertheless, the parties may agree that terrorist actions will be exempted from coverage. In the absence of such agreement, though, such actions are covered. Fire caused by natural deterioration of the insured products is also excluded from coverage.

152. A common clause in fire insurance policies provides that if the insured is prosecuted before criminal courts for causing the fire, the insurer is not obliged to pay the insurance money before the insured's eventual release by the criminal court.

Causing a fire can constitute a criminal offence under the Penal Code, even in the absence of intent, if the fire was caused through gross negligence.

153. Pursuant to a typical clause inserted in fire policies, the insurer is not liable for default interest prior to the criminal court's acquittal. The Supreme Court of Cassation upheld this clause in a case where an express clause on payment of interest was provided in the fire policy.

§2. Commencement and Extent of Coverage

154. Unless otherwise agreed, coverage begins at noon of the day following the conclusion of the contract. However, the parties may agree for coverage to begin immediately upon conclusion of the contract. As mentioned above, the date of conclusion is the date of parties' agreement, which does not necessarily coincide with the date the policy was issued. It is irrelevant whether the day following conclusion is a working day.

155. Unless something else has been agreed, fire coverage includes losses caused by an explosion and other similar events, even if no fire occurred thereafter. The compensation shall cover the reduction in the value of items damaged, as well as expenses incurred in measures taken to ascertain, avert or limit the damage caused, such as expenses relating to extinguishing the fire or demolition of the property. If there is no agreement to the contrary, the insurance also includes losses arising from theft, or losses at the time of the occurrence of the risk or immediately thereafter, or those arising from the emergency measures taken to deal with the fire.

156. The law provides that fire insurance includes coverage for fire-related risks, such as explosion, thunder, earthquake and flood, irrespective of whether they resulted in fire. Thus, if these risks are not expressly excluded, the fire policy covers such losses. Damages from fire and related risks caused by terrorist action are covered unless they are explicitly excluded by the policy.

§3. Scope of Application of Special Fire Insurance Provisions

157. Risks related to fire can be covered by virtue of relevant special provisions included in the fire policy. Coverage of some other risks, such as earthquake and flood, is governed by ICA's provision on fire insurance, applied *mutatis mutandis*. This is because ICA does not regulate all kinds of insurance which fall under indemnity insurance, but only the main ten kinds. Thus, in the non-specially regulated kinds of non-life insurance, ICA's special rules apply *mutatis mutandis*. In line with the classification of insurance into classes and subclasses or risks, i.e., from a supervisory standpoint, the licence issued by the Supervisor of Insurance for the taking up of fire insurance business enables the conduct of insurance against other risks (subclasses) such as explosion, storm and similar natural phenomena, nuclear energy and soil recession. However, only the risk included in the subclass 'fire' is directly regulated by ICA's provision on fire insurance.

If the loss occurred due to the insured's slight negligence, the ICA provides that the insurer will not be released from his obligation to pay the insurance money. Persons concluding insurance for business purposes are free to conclude fire insurance on terms other than those specified in the ICA, including those releasing the insurer from his liability only in cases of malicious conduct or gross negligence. This rule constitutes one of the five exceptional cases where the policy can validly deviate from ICA's provisions to the detriment of the insured if the latter concludes the insurance for business purposes.

Chapter 2. Business Interruption and Loss of Profits Insurance

158. Business interruption insurance is specially regulated by Article 24 of the ICA. In the absence of an agreement to the contrary, it includes loss of profits, actual expenses arising from the occurrence of the risk and consequent expenses arising from the complete or partial interruption of business following the occurrence of the insured risk, such as fire or machinery failure. Consequent expenses include the salary and wages of officers, executives, etc.

The period for which cover is provided must be stated in the policy.

Coverage of the risk of business interruption requires a system for the calculation of losses and profits, consistent with international standards.

Chapter 3. Transport Insurance

§1. General Remarks

159. Transport insurance covers loss, damages or delays in deliveries of goods during transport. Insurance of goods in transit is commonly known as 'marine', even though it does not include exclusively insurance for carriage by sea but also by all means of transport.

There are four kinds of transport insurance. Carriage of goods: (a) by sea, regulated by the CPML and special international treaties; (b) by air, governed by the Code of Private Aviation Law and special international treaties; (c) by railway; and (d) by road, governed by the Code of Commerce and special laws. In addition, the general provision of Article 20 of the ICA is supplementarily applied to all kinds of coverage of goods.

160. Transport insurance does not cover risks threatening the means of transport itself but only those affecting goods in transit. Coverage is provided for the period starting from the moment the carrier acquires the right to dispose the goods for carriage until the carrier loses its disposal right due to the termination of such transportation. Thus, under the ICA, coverage does not necessarily begin from the carrier's receipt of the goods, nor ends with their delivery to the consignee. The person bearing the risk of damage to goods during transit is the party with an interest in concluding transport insurance. For instance, if the consignor is the seller under an 'ex-works' clause, the consignee bears the risks of transport and is entitled to conclude transport insurance in his name and on his own behalf. The insurable interest does not necessarily relate to the owner of the goods. In a 'c.i.f.' (cost, insurance and freight) sale, the seller must, among other contractual obligations, conclude transport insurance and pay the premium.

161. The carrier is another party with an interest in concluding transport insurance, since, if the goods are damaged or lost, or if their delivery is delayed, the carrier is liable to pay compensation. However, although the carrier is not liable under all circumstances for the above events, transport insurance covers all these events under broader circumstances. There are circumstances under which the carrier can be released from his obligation to pay indemnity, while cargo insurance provides coverage to the insured in cases where the carrier is released from his liability as well. Under cargo insurance, the insured loses his right to coverage only if valid objections arising from insurance law are raised, whereas coverage does not depend on objections associated with carrier's liability. Thus, the premium charged for carrier's liability insurance is in principle cheaper than that of cargo transport insurance, by reference to the same voyage and the same goods, since coverage is limited accordingly.

162. If the goods during the transport sustain loss or damage or their delivery is delayed and the transport insurer pays the corresponding insurance money, the latter is subrogated to the insured's rights against the carrier, unless the latter can provide evidence that such claim is not lawfully grounded.

In carriage of goods by sea, the carrier is compulsorily covered by special liability insurance. Usually, the carrier's liability insurance coverage is granted by mutual protection and indemnity (P & I) clubs which commonly operate under Anglo-Saxon law and whose seat is usually outside Greece.

Air carriers of persons and goods are required to conclude compulsory liability insurance, whereas this is not the case with road and rail transport carriers.

§2. Extent of Coverage

163. The ICA provides for in Article 20.4 that, in the case of insurance of carriage of goods, the insurance money is calculated in accordance with the current value of the goods or, in the absence of such a valuation, based on the usual value which the goods had at the place where they were received for carriage. This value may increase by the addition of freight costs, customs' duties and miscellaneous related charges, as well as the anticipated freight. Therefore, overinsurance will exist not simply when the actual value is lower than the value mentioned in the policy but when the value in the policy exceeds the actual value of the goods plus transportation costs. If the policy does not provide that coverage includes also the anticipated profit, the value agreed in the policy cannot be taken to include this amount. Of course, the content of the policy does not confer rights and obligations but serves as proof thereof (documents ad probationem, *see* paragraph 107). Thus, if such an agreement has been reached but has not been included in the policy, the insured does not lose his right to coverage for the anticipated profit. In practice, the policy does not ordinarily refer to coverage of anticipated profits.

A temporary interruption of the carriage, such as a change in the agreed route or means of transport, does not release the insurer from his obligation if such changes were necessary. For the consequences of deviations in a sea-route, *see* paragraph 192.

164. In the carriage of goods by sea, the insurance covers the actual value of the goods at the time when coverage began, that is their value at the place of loading. Loading and discharge costs, freight costs and insurance premiums are the only expenses which are included in the insurance money by law. Any remaining expenses can be covered but only upon specific agreement. Other losses of the insured, such as anticipated profit, can likewise be covered. When such agreements have the form of an 'agreed value' contract (*see* paragraph 202), the policy is called 'value policy'. A value policy may be issued for any transport insurance contract.

According to the CPML, Article 268 paragraph 2, 'the amount of the indemnity shall be the valuation agreed by the parties, provided such valuation is expressly accepted by the insurer in the policy'. However, this provision is not *ius cogens.*

Chapter 4. Liability Insurance

§1. Civil Liability Insurance

165. Civil liability insurance is regulated by Articles 25 and 26 of the ICA. If civil liability is directly related to a sea voyage, it belongs to the broader field of marine insurance since Article 259 CPML provides that any lawful interest exposed to marine risks may constitute the subject matter of marine insurance. This provision also includes civil liability risk. Thus, claims arising out of marine liability insurance are subject to a two years' prescription period, instead of the four years' limitation period applicable to non-marine insurance claims.

The CPML contains no provisions on marine liability insurance, except for a single article on hull coverage which provides that the hull insurer shall be liable for the damages for which the shipowner is liable towards third parties because of collision, except for damages on account of bodily injury or injury to health (Article 269.2 CPML). Shipowners' civil liability for collision is automatically covered by this insurance. The parties may, however, agree to deviate from this rule.

166. In civil liability insurance, the insurer bears all the financial consequences arising from the insured's liability for its acts and omissions described in the policy.

Hence, the civil liability insurer provides coverage of both the legal expenses incurred by the insured for the defence and settlement of third parties' claims and of the amount owed by the insured to the injured third party as indemnity.

Where liability insurance is shaped as compulsory, the third party has a right of direct action against the insurer, up to the insured amount or the minimum sum prescribed by law for the type of compulsory insurance applicable, whichever is higher. The insurer may not raise an objection against the third party based on his contractual relationship with the insured, unless the third party is the policyholder, any other person whose civil liability is covered, or is related to the insured or the policyholder.

167. In general liability insurance, the risk materializes not the moment when the third party suffers the loss – since he may never claim indemnity or claim such indemnity only at a later stage – but at the moment when the third party submits his claim, judicially or extrajudicially; at this point of time, the insured's claim against the insurer for legal expenses arises. A standard clause to be found in liability insurance policies provides that the insured is not entitled to satisfy the third party without the approval or, at least, prior information of the insurer.

The insured's claim against the insurer is time-barred according to the general provision on prescription of all non-life insurance claims, namely after a period of four years, beginning at the end of the year it arose. The insurer's obligation to provide coverage may last a long time, in the sense that, in case of lengthy court proceedings, the insurer's exact extent of liability will eventually be defined upon issuance of the relevant decision.

'Claims made' policies are not regulated by the law. However, case law declares 'claims made' clauses as abusive and unfair and therefore null and void if coverage is restricted only to claims made during the course of the policy's term, without any reasonable extension (reporting period) or if, in the case of policy's renewal with the same insurer, such renewal is made on condition that claims submitted after the policy's extension are not covered.

§2. Professional Liability Insurance

168. Professional liability insurance provides extensive coverage of builders' and engineers' tortious liability and of the contractual liability of doctors, accountants and others. The conclusion of professional civil liability insurance is compulsorily required for, *inter alia*, tour operators and auditors. On the other hand, professional liability insurance covering self-employed activities is a developing field, especially for doctors' professional liability.

169. Error and omission liability insurance of insurance brokers was introduced in 1993. Insurance brokers must obtain liability insurance covering their professional civil liability, unless such insurance is already provided by the insurance undertaking on whose behalf they are acting.

170. Builders' liability insurance falls under two categories according to insurance practice: one category concerns constructors of smaller works where insurance covers liability for damages caused to third parties during construction; this category covers tortious liability and is concluded on a voluntary basis. The other category refers to large and complicated construction works and covers contractual liability but concerns only a small number of cases. In most cases falling within the second category, the extent and terms of coverage are imposed by the employer as part of the contract for work. In these cases, insurers usually provide coverage under strict conditions. For instance, they do not cover contractual liability due to negligence (*see* paragraph 238 on Technical Insurance).

Another well-known liability insurance is the civil liability of the employer for accidents at work, which is examined in detail under Part V, Chapter 1 below.

§3. Product Liability Insurance

171. Special provisions on strict product liability have been in force in Greece since 1980s. However, product liability insurance which covers such liability is not that widespread. Compulsory coverage of such liability does not exist. However, industrial and semi-industrial products made in Greece are almost always covered by special product liability insurance. Case law is not particularly rich, but there are several decisions of the Supreme Court of Cassation. As in all other non-compulsory non-liability insurance, the injured party has no right of direct action against the product liability insurer of the producer.

Article 6 of Law 2251/1994 on consumer protection regulates product liability in accordance with EC Directive 85/374. The producer is liable for any damage caused by the defective product. The previous law on consumer protection, which also provided for product liability (Law 1961/1991), released the producer from liability if he could establish that when the product was placed in circulation, he did not know nor could not have known the existence of the defect. This provision was contrary to the provisions of Directive 85/374 and was repealed by Law 2251/1994. Currently, no limit to the producer's liability is provided by law.

§4. Environmental Liability Insurance

172. Environmental liability insurance is regulated in very general terms by Article 23 of the ICA. In the absence of an agreement to the contrary, it covers the expenses of restoring the natural environment, including the removal of pollutants and waste products arising from the occurrence of the insured loss. It covers only actual expenses occurred, and only in relation to sudden and unexpected events. The insurer can pay the insurance money exclusively for the coverage of such expenses, in return for precise receipt.

Since the 1980s, the law imposes liability without fault (strict liability) for certain kinds of environmental damage. This expansion of the scope of liability for environmental damage in comparison to that of general civil liability is accompanied by an equal expansion in environmental liability's insurance coverage.

The insertion of strict liability for environmental damage aims at the following:

(a) Avoidance of pollution and general environmental deterioration and adoption of all necessary preventive measures to that effect.
(b) Protection of human health from the various forms of environmental deterioration and pollution.
(c) Promotion of a balanced development within the entire national territory and its particular geographical divisions.
(d) Securing the potential renewal of natural resources and the rational exploitation of non-renewable or scarce resources according to current and future needs and in accordance with environmental protection.
(e) Preservation of the ecological balance of natural ecosystems and safeguarding of their capacity for renewal.

More specifically, the law aims at the protection of soil through the establishment of measures guaranteeing that its exploitation is consistent with its natural characteristics and its productive capacity. The relevant provisions are also intended to protect the surface and subterranean waters which are considered as natural resources and ecosystems, as well as to preserve the overlying atmosphere and conserve areas of importance in terms of biology, ecology, aesthetics or geomorphology. The law is further aimed at protecting beaches and riverbanks and at determining the desirable and permissible quality of natural reservoirs, as well as at delineating allowed disposals of waste.

The general rule in Greece is that general liability insurance policies exclude pollution risks, and there is, therefore, no record of application of this type of insurance. Such risks are only exceptionally covered on condition that there is adequate reinsurance coverage. In this case, conditions and exceptions are similar to those set by leading international reinsurance companies.

Coverage of liability for clean-up and/or removal of polluted or contaminated surfaces, regardless of whether it is concluded upon demand of a third party on the basis of general tort law, etc., can be also provided by way of special clauses in general liability policies or pursuant to a specific clause to this effect in fire policies.

Since 2009, Greek law has harmonized its provisions with Directive 2004/35/EC, known as the 'Environmental Liability Directive' (ELD), which imposed expanded the scope of strict liability to a large number of undertakings for certain cases of environmental pollution. The Greek market has developed only recently special insurance products covering ELD liability.

Chapter 5. Legal Expenses Insurance

173. Legal expenses insurance covers the risk of an increase in the insured's liabilities due to judicial or extrajudicial expenses incurred due to the pursuit of a legal claim, court expenditures or the expenses of refuting an unfounded claim. Legal expenses' insurance is not regulated by specific provisions of the ICA. The law on insurance undertakings, fully harmonized with the EU law, includes two particular provisions, one on legal expenses' insurance policies and another on companies conducting such business.

The insurance company must take any necessary measures to prevent its legal expenses' activities from interfering with its activities which fall within the scope of other insurance classes. The law provides a special procedure for pursuing these activities.

174. There are mainly two kinds of risks covered by legal expenses insurance: one concerns legal defence expenses and the other relates to the expenses of filing a lawsuit.

175. Legal expenses insurance undertaken as coverage of a stand-alone risk is essentially different from any other kind of insurance. The loss occurs when the insured decides, with the insurer's approval, that all the conditions for the exercise of his juridical rights are met. This is not the case with liability insurance, whereby the risk occurs when the injured third party raises a claim against the insured, even when the latter also encompasses coverage of the legal expenses incurred in defence of the claim. In this last case, liability insurance also encompasses legal expenses' coverage since, if the insurer doubts the legal basis of the third party's claims against the insured, he consequently proceeds to a trial at his own cost but in the insured's name. These expenses are covered as an ancillary obligation of the liability insurer, so that they cannot be treated as constituting part of combined insurance of two separate risks (liability and legal expenses). Thus, liability insurance is, partially, legal expenses' insurance. A separate licence is required from the Supervisor of Insurance for the taking up of legal expenses' insurance when such insurance is written independently and not as part of liability insurance.

The legal prerequisites for the taking up and pursuit of legal expenses' insurance do not apply to the taking up and pursuit of civil liability insurance when the latter includes coverage of legal expenses for defence against third-party claims.

As mentioned above, civil liability insurance includes coverage of legal defence expenses, the latter being an ancillary obligation of the insurer. Thus, legal expenses' insurance is concluded either in the complete absence of civil liability insurance or in cases where the existing civil liability insurance contract precludes coverage of legal defence expenses. Notably, exclusion of legal defence expenses from coverage is not permissible in compulsory third-party motor insurance.

176. Even in the case of compulsory motor insurance, though, the insurer can only cover legal expenses proportional to the extent of liability. The injured third party can be covered for the remainder by a separate legal expenses' insurance contract. Coverage of expenses for legal defence is not considered as an ancillary risk.

Legal expenses' insurance coverage includes expenses incurred in defence against criminal actions but never extends to pecuniary sanctions imposed by courts or administrative authorities. However, in case the insured is condemned, he is obliged to return the insurance money received so far.

The performance of the legal expenses' insurer is not confined to the coverage of legal aid expenses but may also cover legal consultation.

177. An essential principle of the law is the insured's freedom in choosing his lawyer. A basic distinction is made between providing legal services and providing legal expenses' insurance. The former, according to mandatory provisions, may be provided only by members of the bars. The insurer cannot, therefore, offer legal advice, but may only pay the expenses for such advice.

The legal expenses' insurer cannot appoint an attorney of his own accord for the insured's legal affairs; he may only recommend lawyers, on the insured's request. The insurer is only burdened with the expenses and has no responsibility for the outcome of the case.

In the event of a dispute between the insurer and the insured concerning the need for the latter's protection before administrative or judicial authorities, the insured may demand the issue of a legal opinion by any jurist he chooses. If the insurance company disagrees with the contents of the opinion, the dispute is submitted to arbitration.

Chapter 6. Marine Insurance

§1. General Principles

I. The Insurable Interest

178. Marine insurance is regulated in more detail than non-marine/non-life insurance. As with aviation insurance (*see* paragraphs 220 et seq.), provisions on marine insurance contain the same principles which apply to all kinds of non-life insurance. From the point of view of the distinction made above (under paragraph 93) between sum and indemnity insurance, marine insurance falls under indemnity insurance. Consequently, the rules that apply to fixed sum insurance do not apply to marine insurance, which is regulated by the principles of indemnity insurance, such as subrogation and the prohibition of overinsurance.

The Greek CPML, which, as mentioned above, contains the provisions on marine insurance contract under Title 14 (Articles 257–288), provides for in Article 257 that Articles 189–225 on insurance contracts, included in the Commercial Code (now replaced by the ICA), shall also apply in the case of navigation risks unless they are incompatible with marine insurance. Thus, the ICA provisions on non-life insurance contracts apply *mutatis mutandis*. However, while acts which limit the rights of the insured beyond the limitations expressly set out in the ICA are void, this provision does not apply to marine insurance policies (Article 33 of the ICA). As mentioned above (paragraph 27), the Greek CPML replaced the Second Book of the Commercial Code on Maritime Commerce which had already been amended in 1910.

179. Marine insurance covers all interests exposed to marine risks, even though marine risks do not necessarily originate directly from the sea. It is sufficient, therefore, that these are indirectly related to the sea. Examples of such risks are the fire risk which caused damages to a vessel and/or its cargo or the machinery breakdown risk. The importance of the definition of insurance as marine or non-marine lies in the different configurations contained in Greek maritime law (14th title of CPML), on the one hand, and the provisions of general insurance contract law (ICA), on the other hand. An important difference between these two sets of rules concerns prescription, which is four years for non-marine insurance claims and two years for marine insurance claims (*see* paragraph 165).

As far as premium's payment is concerned, there is a special provision applicable in marine insurance, providing for payment of the total premium if insurance cover has begun, while only half the premium is payable if the risk has been eliminated before the commencement of coverage.

II. The Principle of 'All-Risks'

180. Contrary to non-marine insurance, marine insurance is governed by the principle of all risks. This principle, namely coverage of all risks without specification of each particular risk provided that such risks can be characterized as marine insurance risks, is not a mandatory principle and, consequently, contractual deviations are valid. In fact, it is common practice to strictly define and, therefore, drastically limit the scope of covered marine risks through a relevant clause included in the policy's general terms. Another common method of restricting the all-risks' nature of marine insurance is to introduce exceptions to the risks or to include warranties. According to theory, the all-risks' principle is a characteristic apparent in all transport insurance rather than an exclusive characteristic of marine insurance.

181. The CPML provides in Article 259 that any lawful interest, including an anticipated profit, may form the subject matter of marine insurance. Coverage does not, therefore, extend to unlawful interests. In the context of marine insurance, 'lawful interest' does not have the dual meaning it bears in non-marine insurance, where it comprises both the economic bond and the legal interest in avoiding the risk, which the person requesting coverage must possess. 'Interest' here means the economic bond between the insured and the asset, in other words, the objective value of the asset, while the asset's subjective value for the insured can also be taken into account, according to a view. Nevertheless, the 'interest' in the former sense is also apparent in marine insurance as a result of the complementary application of non-marine insurance provisions to such contracts. For example, a person may conclude a hull insurance contract in his name for a ship which continuously engages in the transport of goods, as either the shipper or the consignee of such goods, since he has an interest in the preservation and safe transportation of the goods. In this case, the insurance contract functions as insurance for the benefit of the shipowner. It is important that the insured in both marine and non-marine insurance must have a legal interest in avoiding the risk.

III. Multiple or Double Insurance

182. The ICA has repealed the difference in the treatment of multiple/double insurance between marine and non-marine insurance provided for under previous legislation; the rule in both is that, whenever the same interest is insured more than once, each insurance is valid up to the value of the interest and the insurers are jointly and severally liable. In case of fraud, the relevant rule of non-marine insurance applies; the insurer is released from his obligation to pay the insurance money, so that the insured who has fraudulently concluded overinsurance in the form of double insurance is deprived of the benefit of insurance.

IV. Limitation

183. Claims arising out of a marine insurance contract are subject to two-years' prescription, the limitation period commencing from the end of the year in which the claim arose. A differentiation is thereby introduced, as in marine insurance the limitation period is two years, while in non-marine indemnity insurance, it is four years. In both cases (marine and non-marine insurance), the rules of the Civil Code on the interruption of limitation also apply (i.e., limitation is interrupted mainly upon serving of a lawsuit or in case of acknowledgement of the claim by the debtor). The limitation is also interrupted when a declaration of abandonment of the goods is served to the insurer.

§2. Marine Insurance Law and Policy Terms

I. The Influence of English Law

184. The detailed provisions of Greek law on marine insurance are of rather limited practical importance. Marine insurance written by Greek insurers includes, as a rule, insurance clauses shaped by international marine insurance institutions, while it is accompanied by extensive reinsurance coverage, written abroad. These two factors have led to the broad use of the general terms of the Institute of London Underwriters. This satisfies the reinsurers' wish to be familiar with the conditions precedent to the undertaken risks' coverage and also the insureds' desire to obtain coverage through policies containing widely used terms. However, this practice assigns secondary importance to Greek marine insurance law as its application is not mandatory and the policy may provide otherwise. Although the application of Greek marine insurance law is confined to only few of the contracts concluded, the provisions of general Greek insurance law remain applicable as mandatory law.

II. The 'Free of Particular Average' Clause

185. The 'free of particular average' clause of the policy releases the insurer from any liability arising from loss or damage which does not constitute a total loss or a case of abandonment. It is, therefore, irrelevant whether there is a 'free of partial average' clause in the policy. The insurer's release includes both damage and lack of delivery of the cargo.

III. War Risk

186. Ordinarily, in marine insurance coverage of war risks is excluded, unless otherwise provided in the policy. If coverage includes war risks, the insurance covers losses resulting from any act or event of war and also from any event which occurred after the end of a war but attributable thereto. Risks of civil war and uprisings are treated as war risks. Risks related to terrorist actions are never treated as war risks, unless they can be characterized as such according to the above regulations.

As to valuation, the agreement may not be contested on the grounds of error.

§3. Duration of the Marine Insurance Contract

I. Beginning and Duration of Coverage

187. The rule on the duration of the marine insurance contract deviates from the corresponding rules on non-marine insurance. If time insurance has been concluded, coverage begins from the date of issue of the policy. If the time period is measured in weeks, it expires after the corresponding day of the last week has elapsed. If it is measured in months, it expires after the corresponding date of the last month has elapsed, or, if there is no such date, after the lapse of the last day of the last month. The time period calculated in years expires after the lapse of the corresponding date of the last year. Time periods of half a month are taken to mean fifteen days.

188. A day is considered to last from midnight to midnight of the next day. Further, time is always the local time of the country where the policy is issued. The risk on the first and last days is borne by the insurer. In spite of the above, if the period of insurance expires during a voyage, it is extended to the day following the day when the ship anchors and ties up at the port of its final destination. The insurer is entitled to a proportionate additional premium (*see* more on the duration of insurance coverage below under hull insurance, cargo and freight insurance, paragraphs 202–211.)

189. Cargo insurance begins upon commencement of loading and especially the moment the insured goods cease to touch dry land while it ends the moment they are landed at the port of destination and, in any event, thirty days after the arrival of the ship at that port. Coverage continues for such time as the goods remain in lighters in accordance with local custom.

190. If the risk commences, the full premium is due. If, for any reason, the risk fails to commence, an amount equal to half the premium is due. The amount may in no case exceed 0.5% of the insured sum.

II. Termination of the Marine Insurance Contract

191. The marine insurance contract covering normal marine risks is terminated as soon as the ship enters a situation of war, provided that no special coverage of such was agreed upon. If the situation of war is entered during a voyage, the contract is terminated when the ship reaches the first port. Even though the risk of war is excluded from coverage, war as a real situation may, nevertheless, bring losses covered by the insurance contract.

In the case of 'time insurance', the insurer who has terminated the contract returns the part of the unearned premium.

§4. Basic Particular Obligations of the Contracting Parties

I. The Insured

192. There are some variations in the insured's obligations towards the insurer, which concern mainly deviations in the sea route, damages caused by the fault of the crew, etc., and the costs of navigation.

A. Deviations from the Ship's Prearranged Itinerary

193. The insurer is released from the obligation of coverage if the insured effects any change to the route, the voyage or the ship. The insurer remains, however, entitled to the premium. The replacement of the ship's master does not itself release the insurer from its obligations.

B. Damages Incurred by Fault of the Crew, Etc.

194. Damages due to the fault of the master, the crew or other persons do not release the insurer from its obligations.

C. Costs of Navigation

195. Costs of navigation, entering a port, lying in a port, quarantine or duties, pertaining to the ship or the cargo do not burden the insurer.

D. Obligations after the Loss Occurs

196. After the loss occurs, the insured must provide the insurer with all relevant information. The insured is liable to compensate the insurer if he fails to comply with the above obligation.

II. Payment of the Insurance Money

A. Liability of the Insurer

197. The insurer is liable for losses arising from any event occurring during the voyage, including theft. The insurer is liable for damages incurred to third parties because of collision. Nevertheless, in the absence of an agreement to the contrary, the insurer is not required to cover damages due attributed to bodily injury or deterioration of health.

B. Calculation of the Insurance Money

198. The insurance money is determined by the value of the insured property when the coverage begins. In the case of insured cargo, loading and discharge costs are added, as are the freight and insurance premium. If the valuation of the indemnity is agreed by the parties, the policy must contain the insurer's express acceptance of such valuation since, under Greek law, the agreed value is regarded as an extra contract included in the policy and not as a simple clause of the policy.

§5. Categories of Marine Insurance

I. General Remarks

199. The best known and most widespread kinds of marine insurance coverage offered by the Greek market are hull, cargo and freight insurance. Liability insurance is also subject to the specific provisions on marine insurance when the claim against the insured is connected with sea voyages. In practice, however, such business is usually conducted by P&I clubs, to which Greek law does not apply.

On the other hand, life insurance is governed by ICA's rules, even when the risk is related to the sea. This is important for the application of the ICA's non-marine insurance provisions, including the provisions on prescription which differ from the respective provisions of marine insurance. In non-marine, non-life insurance, the limitation period is four years commencing from the end of the calendar year, in which the claim arose, while in marine insurance the limitation period is two years initiating from the end of the calendar year, in which the claim arose.

II. Crew Insurance

200. Crew insurance is often written in Greece. Marine insurance provisions do not apply if the crew insurance has been concluded not as indemnity but as fixed sum insurance. The fixed sum insurance of the crew is usually concluded by the shipowner in the form of group insurance, namely for the benefit of the crew, and entails payment of a lump sum in case of death or total/partial, permanent/temporary disability arising from accident or illness. Consequently, the beneficiary is exclusively the member of the crew or his/her heirs or a third-party beneficiary, appointed by the insured in case of death insurance.

Crew insurance may also function as indemnity insurance (accident and illness insurance). In this case, ICA's provisions on non-marine insurance apply, instead of CPML's provisions regulating marine insurance contracts. Eventual payment of indemnity to seamen by the social insurer and/or by the damaging third party does not affect the private insurer's obligation to pay the insurance money since despite the conclusion of crew insurance as indemnity insurance, it may be accumulated with social insurance. In this respect, non-marine insurance principles apply to every kind of insurance for bodily injury or death caused by events related to marine risks, namely, the principles of accumulation of insurance money and indemnity from other sources as well as the absence of the private insurer's right to subrogation.

As regards passengers, there was until recently a special kind of compulsory insurance for damages or death written by the Seamen's Pension Fund which has been abolished (*see* paragraph 52).

III. Shipowner's Liability Insurance

201. Shipowner's liability insurance for accidents of the crew is written mainly to cover claims for moral damages. The crew is compulsorily covered by social insurance: as mentioned already, social insurance replaces the employer's civil liability, except for the liability for moral damages. There would be no such replacement if the accident was the result of the employer's reckless actions and with the knowledge that damages could probably result. In this case, both the social insurer and the shipowner are liable. In marine insurance of persons, we have an accumulation of the indemnity paid by the Seamen's Pension Fund, the indemnity eventually paid by the person who caused the accident, and the insurance money paid by the private insurer. As in non-marine insurance, the liability insurer of the shipowner covers the claims of the injured seaman for moral damages because those damages are not covered by the Fund. The Fund does not replace the shipowner's liability for moral damages.

Liability insurance is not included in the all-risks' notion of marine insurance; i.e., coverage of liability must be expressly agreed upon to be included in marine insurance policy's scope, with the sole exception of liability for damage to property caused by the collision of vessels.

IV. Hull Insurance

202. Hull insurance operates as indemnity insurance. Coverage is extended to all damages of the ship, as well as to liability due to collision. Not only the shipowner but also anyone with a lawful interest in avoiding the risk is entitled to take out such insurance, such as the person managing the ship on his own account based on an agreement with the owner.

203. The ship's value agreed upon which is the basis for the calculation of the insurance money is usually not the actual value of the vessel and its compartments but its agreed value. The common practice in Greek hull insurance is to conclude a contract for the value of the vessel (agreed value policies) with the purpose of avoiding underinsurance or overinsurance of the ship.

204. The CPML provides (Article 85) that the shipowner shall be released from liability for the master's legal acts made during the performance of the duties delegated to him and for the unlawful acts committed by the crew or the pilot or the master in the performance of the duties entrusted to them upon surrender of the ship and the gross freight. Surrender does not include insurance benefits except for claims arising out of accidental harm to persons.

205. A special rule is used to calculate the duration of insurance coverage if the ship is insured under a voyage policy: coverage begins from the commencement of the loading or the taking on of ballast and ends upon discharge. Where a new voyage policy follows immediately after the previous one, cover in respect of the previous voyage shall cease upon commencement of cover under the new policy.

V. Cargo and Freight Insurance

A. General Remarks

206. As mentioned above, cargo insurance is classified as marine insurance concluded for a certain time period (time insurance) or for a certain voyage (voyage insurance). The insurance sum is calculated according to the value of the goods at the time of loading, plus loading and discharge expenses, the freight and the insurance premium.

B. Open Cover

207. The CPML provides for a special kind of marine insurance (which can also be concluded as non-marine insurance): floating or open or general insurance. This kind of insurance covers the consigned goods for a certain period of time and for a certain amount, without specifying, like other kinds of insurance, other factors such as the means of transport, the exact description of the goods, the place of consignment and the place of loading. Floating or open insurance qualifies as future interest insurance. The insured is obliged to notify the insurer on the above factors, as soon as the insured becomes aware of them, so that the premium may be calculated. If there is no such notification, the insurer may claim damages from the insured. Nevertheless, it can also be concluded that the above notification is optional or that the contract is declared null and void and the insurer is released from the obligation to pay the insurance money as a sanction for the insured's failure to notify.

C. Anticipated Profit

208. The anticipated profit and/or the rise in the cargo's value at its destination compared to its value at the place of loading can be insured under a marine insurance policy from the arrival of the cargo at its destination. This insurance covers the risk of loss of the anticipated profit, which is indirectly subject to sea risks.

D. Transhipment of Goods

209. If the ship becomes unseaworthy, the costs of goods' transhipment, storage, custody, excess freight and salvage burden the insurer, up to the amount of the sum insured.

E. Bearer of the Insurable Interest

210. In cargo insurance, the lawful possession of the insurance policy and the bill of lading constitute sufficient proof that their holder is the bearer of the insurable interest. The insurer may not invoke non-payment of the premium and consequent release from his obligations against the new owner in case of transfer of the policy and the bill of lading unless the latter acts in bad faith.

The above rule applies *mutatis mutandis* in cases of alienation owing to forced sale.

F. Freight Insurance

211. Furthermore, a marine insurance policy can also cover the risk of loss of the freight due to an accident or to another sea event which caused the carriage to be cancelled. In this case, the provisions of the insurance of ships apply if the risk is borne by the carrier. The provisions on cargo insurance apply if the risk is borne by the freighter. The freight insured is the gross freight, on condition that the costs of supplies, wages of the crew are paid in advance and insurance premiums are not separately covered.

§6. Insurance of Mortgaged Ship

212. If there is a mortgage on the vessel securing a creditor's claim, then the mortgage is extended to the insurance money. In the event of damage to the vessel, the creditor whose rights are secured by the mortgage has a right of direct claim against the insurer.

The exact actual value of the hull (including the value of its components and accessories which are also subject to this kind of insurance) is not taken into account for the payment of the insurance money if it is calculated on the basis of the agreed value contract. This procedure is quite common in hull insurance and helps the parties rebut objections of overinsurance and underinsurance.

213. The CPML (Article 198) provides that the mortgagee, in the absence of the vessel's marine insurance, shall be entitled, at the mortgagor's expense, to insure the ship against marine risks, the insured sum not exceeding the debt's value increased by 30%. Nevertheless, interpretation suggests that this configuration cannot lead to the vessel's overinsurance for more than 30% of its value. The rights conferred by the mortgage shall also be exercisable over the insurance money.

Furthermore, Article 190 para 3 of the CPML provided that the debtor shall be bound to manage and operate the ship diligently and in accordance with proper operating standards, while Article 194 pronounces that 'if the ship is lost or sustains damage which substantially reduces its value, the creditor shall be entitled to demand immediate satisfaction of his/her debt. No such right shall exist if the damage is not attributed to the debtor's fault and the latter offers adequate security thereto'. It is noted that the provisions of both Article 190, para 3 and Article 194 of the CPML apply to ship mortgages, as well.

§7. Abandonment of the Insured Interest to the Insurer

214. In hull, cargo and freight insurance, the law entitles the insured to abandon, under certain conditions, the insured object to the insurer and claim the entire insurance money. The aforementioned insured's right can be exercised if the ship is lost or is no longer seaworthy due to a shipping incident or if its damages are irreparable. Moreover, if the costs of raising and repairing the ship exceed three-quarters of the ship's value, or if three months elapse without news of the ship, or in the case of seizure, the insured can submit a statement to the insurer declaring his intention to abandon the ship, obliging thus the insurer to pay the entire sum insured. The insurance contract must be valid in order for the insured to proceed with the declaration of abandonment.

215. If within thirty days from service of the abandonment declaration to the insurer the latter does not contest the insured's right of abandonment or if such right is recognized judicially, the rights over the abandoned ship are transferred to the insurer. The transfer is deemed to have been completed as of the transmittal of the declaration of abandonment. The insured must equip the insurer with any information known to him and deliver any documentary evidence in his possession. In case of coverage for anticipated profits, the insurer acquires no rights from abandonment.

The insurer has the right to refuse to acquire ownership of the property abandoned, provided that, at the same time, he unconditionally undertakes to pay the insurance money in full. On the other hand, the insurer is entitled to call upon the insured to abandon the insured object within a reasonable time, stipulated by the former. If such period expires without any action having been taken, the insured forfeits the right of abandonment.

216. Case law has dealt with the question of whether the insurer's silence on the insured's declaration of abandonment equates to acceptance of such declaration. The proper approach, being in line with Articles 283 ff. of the CPML regulating the abandonment's procedure, suggests that no binding conclusions as to the insurer's intentions should be derived from the mere fact of his silence. The insurer's overall behaviour must be taken into account for the assessment of whether silence equates to refusal of the declaration of abandonment. In conclusion, the insurer's express acceptance of the declaration of abandonment is not required, while the absence of its express denial does not necessarily connote its approval.

Therefore, the insurer's refusal to acknowledge the insured's damage as soon as it occurs, because of, for instance, the insured's failure to pay the premiums or breach of essential insurance terms or warranties entails the subsequent refusal to accept the insured's declaration of abandonment, so that it is unnecessary to repeat the refusal of such declaration if the insurer has already refused the entire claim in advance or has expressed reservations regarding his obligation to provide coverage.

§8. Alienation of the Insured Interest

I. General Remarks

217. If the insured interest is alienated, including alienation by compulsory auction, the rights and obligations arising out of the insurance contract are transferred to the new owner.

II. Alienation of a Vessel

218. In the case of hull insurance, the new owner shall be liable for the premium jointly and severally with the previous owner. The former shall be entitled to terminate the contract within one month from the alienation, in which case he shall not be liable for the premium. The insurer shall be released from his obligations in case of materialization of the risk pursuant to events which would not have occurred if the alienation had not taken place.

III. Alienation of Cargo

219. The cargo insurer cannot invoke release from his obligations based on non-payment of the premium against the new owner, provided that the latter acts in good faith.

Chapter 7. Aviation Insurance

220. Like marine insurance, the aviation insurance contract is concluded as indemnity insurance and not as sum insurance. Special provisions are introduced by the PAC. However, the provisions contained therein are minimal. CPML and ICA apply by way of analogy to aviation insurance, according to an explicit provision embodied in PAC. PAC provides that aviation insurance can cover any lawful interest exposed to aviation risks, including loss of anticipated profit.

221. The aviation insurance contract includes, in particular, aeroplane hull and air cargo insurance. In addition, the conclusion of insurance against air carrier's liability for damages to property (transported goods and luggage) and for death or bodily injury of passengers is compulsory for the air carrier. Air carrier's liability insurance vis-à-vis passengers is concluded on a lump sum basis. Thus, the passenger (or his successors) receives from the air carrier liability insurer a fixed sum which is determined in advance, irrespective of the existence and extent of the particular damage.

Beneficiaries are entitled to collect insurance money from the air carrier's liability insurer, irrespective of whether the passenger himself had already concluded insurance covering the risks of bodily injury or death. The passenger/beneficiary may receive cumulatively indemnity from both insurers (the air carrier's insurer and his insurer) since the insurance money is owed in the form of a fixed sum and is not calculated in accordance with the extent of the damage. If air carrier's liability insurance for passengers' injury or death is concluded, as required by law, on a lump sum basis and covers the entire extent of the air carrier's civil liability, as soon as the passenger receives the insurance money, the air carrier is released from his liability. Thus, such insurance replaces the carrier's liability towards the injured party so far as the claim derives from the insured's special liability in his capacity as an air carrier.

222. The air carrier can conclude either special aviation liability insurance in his name and on his behalf or insurance against the risks of injury or death on behalf of the passengers. In both cases, insurance replaces the special air carrier's liability in terms of compensation's payment: the carrier remains liable but is covered; that is, he is not obliged to pay indemnity. This is different from the situation under employees' social insurance: whatever the extent of the employer's civil liability, he is not liable if the employee is covered by a Social Insurance Fund. The carrier's general liability, though, is not replaced by the existence of the aforesaid special insurance coverage. If the carrier is liable for indemnity owed for reasons other than losses or damages suffered by passengers or loss of their possessions, then he is not covered by the above-mentioned special air carrier's insurance. Thus, from the air carrier's point of view, the distinction between the two kinds of insurance is important when the aviation insurance contract covers general liability. Unless it has been expressly stipulated in the policy that the insurance money payable to the passenger corresponds to the indemnity that the carrier has to pay to the passenger as compensation in view of his liability, in case of a passenger's death or injury, the passenger's claim against the carrier remains intact and may be brought cumulatively with the claim against the insurer and regardless of whether the passenger has already been compensated by the insurer.

Aviation insurance against the risks of passengers' injury or death and damage or loss of transported goods must be compulsorily taken out by the carrier. The law does not stipulate whether the insurance in question should be concluded as liability insurance or as general property insurance. On the other hand, it should be noted that under EU Regulation 785/2004, air carriers are required to compulsorily take out passenger and third-party accident liability insurance as well as luggage, cargo and mail damage insurance.

223. Special terms in the aviation insurance contract, which deviate from the usual general terms used in property insurance policies, are, in particular, the following:

(1) Hull insurance begins on the day of issuance of the policy and not on the day the relevant agreement is reached or the following day, as happens with fire insurance. In voyage hull insurance, coverage begins and ends at the beginning and end of the flight, respectively. When hull insurance provides coverage against losses occurring during a certain period of time specified in the policy – instead of coverage against losses occurring during the term of a voyage – if the period of coverage happens to expire during the term of a flight, then coverage is automatically extended until the end of the flight, upon payment of an additional premium.

(2) If the transported goods are insured, coverage also extends to their voyage by aircraft which was not originally subject to the policy but to which the goods have been transshipped because the original aircraft was unable to continue the voyage.

224. In hull insurance and insurance for the transport of goods, the insured has the right to abandon the insured object to the insurer. In hull insurance, abandonment may take place: (a) if the aircraft is lost or unable to fly and cannot be repaired, (b) if there has been no news of the aircraft for the past fifteen days, and/or (c) if the repair costs exceed three-quarters of the value of the aircraft at the beginning of coverage. In the case of carriage of goods, abandonment is permitted: (a) if the aircraft carrying the goods is lost or there has been no news of the aircraft for the previous fifteen days, and/or (b) if rescuing the goods and transporting them to their destination are impossible or would damage the goods.

225. PAC's special provisions on the duration of aviation insurance, as well as on the content of the insurance policy and the right of abandonment, are not mandatory. However, PAC's provisions on aviation insurance prevail over the general provisions of the ICA since they regulate special matters. The latter applies by way of analogy only if the provisions of aviation insurance law do not regulate specifically the issue in question.

226. The calculation of the insurance money payable for goods in transit is based on the actual value of the goods at the place and time of discharge.

Chapter 8. Theft and Embezzlement Insurance

227. ICA does not specifically regulate theft and embezzlement insurance. The general provisions on insurance contract and on non-life insurance are applicable.

Theft insurance is commonly offered as an ancillary coverage included in fire policies. Theft coverage is also granted in transport and marine insurance within the frame of 'all-risks' coverage. Theft of motor vehicles is covered by motor insurance policies as ancillary coverage of standard policies. General theft insurance policies offered on the Greek market do not include coverage against theft of property in transit or theft of motor vehicles. These special risks are covered by transport insurance policies, marine and motor vehicle policies.

228. Theft and embezzlement insurance are types of indemnity insurance, covering damages to tangible items. They constitute coverages, where the insurance sum is calculated with reference to the actual value of the stolen property. As a rule, loss of profit, commercial damages, insults of personality, rights associated with the insured object's surplus value, damages of intangible goods and, in particular, of industrial property rights, consequential damages and purely 'economic' losses do not fall under theft coverage.

229. Coverage is usually restricted by clauses excluding coverage in case of theft by use of a pass-key and in the case where the insured did not take due care for the protection of the insured object against theft. Under the ICA, lack of due care must connote gross negligence for the insurer to be entitled to refuse coverage. In motor vehicle theft insurance, there is a standard exception clause providing that payment against theft of the whole car is not effected before three months have elapsed from the day it was stolen.

Chapter 9. Agricultural Insurance, Hail Insurance, Livestock Insurance

230. Agricultural insurance covers damages to agricultural products caused by hail, disease, frost, etc. This insurance is not very common in Greece because these risks are usually covered by the Organization of Greek Agricultural Insurance (ELGA). ELGA was established by law in 1988 (Law 1790/1988) as a legal entity of private law wholly owned by the state. Its purpose is to organize and implement projects for the protection and insurance of production and capital of agricultural businesses. In this respect, ELGA replaced the Organisation of Agricultural Insurance, a social security entity which, formerly, also provided insurance cover against certain agricultural production risks. Nevertheless, a considerable field of activity is still left to private insurance, which undertakes to cover the risks exceeding the ceilings applied by social insurance.

231. Agricultural insurance is regulated by the ICA, Article 21. It is provided that the insurance money is calculated on the basis of the value the damaged agricultural products would have had at the time of harvest or ripeness, had the accident not taken place.

232. Natural disasters are excluded from the scope of insurance against common fire policies and related risks. However, there are differentiations associated with the cause that led to the risk's occurrence: for instance, albeit the risk of flood is normally covered, flood resulting from a cyclone is not. Such events may be insured upon a special, extra premium. However, natural disasters are covered by the Organisation of Greek Agricultural Insurance.

Chapter 10. Earthquake Insurance

233. Earthquake, as a special kind of natural disaster, is widely insured in Greece but only in relation to industrial risks. Coverage may be obtained merely for the risk of earthquake or in conjunction with fire insurance.

There is no 'first loss' clause in earthquake insurance (*see* paragraph 125). Business interruption due to earthquake may also be insured. Earthquake insurance is concluded for one year so that an annual premium is also payable for coverage of shorter duration. Premiums are classified into three rates depending on how prone the specific region is to earthquakes and on the degree of anti-earthquake protection infrastructures in the area.

Parliament has been debating as to whether earthquake insurance should become compulsory for buildings, to cover a portion of the damage by way of a 'first loss' policy. Although many relevant Draft Bills have been prepared, no law to this effect has yet been passed. Related discussions continue in Greece since the 1990s.

Chapter 11. Credit and Suretyship Insurance

§1. Credit Insurance

234. Credit insurance is expressly governed by the ICA. Unless expressly agreed to the contrary, credit insurance does not confer the insurer the right to demand that the creditor turns against the principal debtor in the first place.

Credit insurance is quite common; although a creditor's claim is usually secured through mortgages, pledges, etc., there always remains the risk of non-payment, for instance, in the case of debtor's bankruptcy. Considering that in Greece, payment on credit represents a very usual practice, the importance of credit insurance is evident. Furthermore, a credit insurance certificate is a useful document as it reinforces the creditor's financial status and is important for his further business relations.

235. There is specific legislation on export credit. The 'Organisation of Credit Export Insurance' provides guarantees, as well as insurance and reinsurance cover to Greek export companies against the risk of insolvency, default, arbitrary termination or non-performance of the contract, unavoidable alteration in the means of transport, destruction of merchandise during carriage or construction, prohibition of exchange transfers, cancellation of import or export licences by State Authorities, acts of the foreign state which impede the performance of the contract and force majeure, such as war or strikes. The Organization is a legal entity of private law, whose liabilities are guaranteed by the Greek state. The legal relations of export undertakings with the Organization are governed by public law. The provisions on insurance contract do not apply directly but by analogy. There are also other mutual insurance arrangements for export insurance in place on a European and a United Nations' level.

§2. Suretyship Insurance

236. The guarantee entails the risk that the guarantor may be obliged to pay the debt of the debtor towards the creditor being at the same time unable to recover the amount from the debtor.

Suretyship insurance places the insurer in the guarantor's position. The surety insurer offers the creditor a guarantee for his (the creditor's) eventual claim against the debtor. Guarantees for participation in construction works' tender procedures and performance guarantees given by construction companies are examples of this type of insurance.

237. The ICA expressly regulates suretyship insurance (Article 22). Unless agreed otherwise, the insurer retains the right to claim from the principal debtor the sum paid to the creditor under guarantee, in accordance with the terms of the policy. The parties to suretyship insurance policies may legally agree on the restriction of the policyholder's rights. Suretyship insurance does not figure a great deal in the Greek insurance market as it used to be banks' business to act as guarantors in most situations. It is not common for insurance companies to issue letters of guarantee.

Suretyship insurance was recognized as a separate insurance class following the implementation of the EU Directives which entitled insurance companies to take up such business. Greek law enacting the Solvency II Directive contains provisions on credit and suretyship insurance concerning solely the taking up and pursuit of the relevant business and not the operation of the insurance contract: regulations pertain, therefore, to insurance supervision.

Chapter 12. Technical Insurance

238. As far as technical insurance is concerned, the insurance industry offers particular coverage of several risks related, among others, to construction works, plants and machinery, as well as the internationally acknowledged coverages construction all-risks and erection all-risks. From an insurance law perspective, technical insurance can be distinguished into passive (liability insurance) and active technical insurance. Active technical insurance may be further classified as insurance against damages to objects (such as machinery) and as coverage tendered for purely economic damages (such as business interruption).

ICA expressly regulates business interruption insurance (Article 24). Unless otherwise agreed, losses covered under business interruption insurance include loss of profit, general expenses and other costs directly arising from the occurrence of the insured risk.

Part IV. Motor Vehicle Insurance

Chapter 1. Motor Vehicle Liability Insurance: The Legal Regime

§1. General Remarks

239. Motor vehicle liability insurance is treated as liability insurance and also as insurance for damages because it also covers legal defence expenses against the unfounded claims of a third party. Moreover, it is usually purchased along with fire/theft/'own' damage coverage insurance. MTPL insurance is compulsory in Greece since 1976, although non-fault liability for the driver or owner of the car exists since 1911. MTPL covers both non-fault civil liability and civil liability based on fault for damages arising from the use of any kind of motor vehicle on streets and lands freely accessible to the public. It also covers moral damages awarded by Greek Courts which usually adjudicate remarkably high amounts of compensation in cases of personal injuries and, in particular, of death incurred by the motor accident. It is sufficient that the damage was a result of a driver's act, or that it was caused by the operation of the motor vehicle, for the owner of the car or the driver to be declared liable.

§2. Civil Liability for Motor Accidents

240. The Law of 4 December 1911 on civil liability for motor accidents holds the driver, the owner and the possessor of the vehicle (in case the owner is not in possession of the vehicle) responsible for losses, namely either damages to property or bodily injuries, incurred during the circulation of the vehicle, even in the absence of fault. The liability of the above persons is unlimited, with one exception: in cases where the driver is not the owner of the car, the owner is liable up to the value the vehicle had before the accident.

In Greece, there are constant increases in the minimum insured sum to ensure compliance with EU law. As of 1 January 2022, MTPL insurance coverage must compulsorily amount to at least EUR 1,300,000 per victim in case of personal injuries and to EUR 1,300,000 per accident in case of damage to property, regardless of the number of victims. There is no ceiling on the payable insurance money in accordance with the number of accidents the insured has caused within one year.

Coverage encompasses liability of the vehicle's owner as well as the vehicle's possessor, excluding damages caused by a thief or person who acquired hold of the vehicle through use of violence. It does not include civil liability towards passengers who knew that the vehicle was stolen or was being used for unlawful purposes.

General liability policies exclude the MTPL coverage since the latter is always sold as a special policy.

The no-fault liability for motor vehicle accidents does not apply in case of collision and liability for damages caused to goods in transit. In the event of a collision, the liable party is the party at fault. The no-fault rule is also overridden when the injured party is jointly liable, so that the indemnity owed is calculated in proportion to the parties' fault. The owner, driver or possessor of the vehicle is released if he proves that the accident was caused by force majeure or was exclusively attributed to the victim's fault. The driver may be released if he proves that the accident occurred because of a mechanical deficiency in the vehicle which could not have been detected. Even in this case, though, the insurer remains liable but, as a rule, his liability is confined up to the motor vehicle's value.

241. If a third party was jointly at fault for the accident, the party who compensated the victim can recover from that third party up to the extent of the latter's fault. The driver may file an application to join the third party to the proceedings so that the allocation of fault is decided upon in court.

The injured party may bring an action against the parties at fault within five years from the accident. Prescription for the recovery claim mentioned above is also five years, commencing from the date when the liable party compensated the victim and not from the date of the accident.

242. The Greek law on MTPL exclusively includes mandatory rules. Only matters not specifically regulated by this law are covered by general law. In adjudicating on a motor accident case, the Court takes into account the specific circumstances, the existence and degree of each party's fault, the penal character of the parties' actions, the financial status of the victim and the testimony of witnesses to the accident.

§3. Compulsory Liability Insurance

I. Scope of Application

243. The law on compulsory motor vehicle liability insurance, notwithstanding some minor exceptions, does not introduce specific insurance contract rules but only regulates the insurer's obligations in relation to the third party to whom the insured caused damage, as well as establishes the obligation of the car owner to conclude insurance amounting to the minimum coverage provided therein. The third party is entitled to bring an action directly against the insurer, irrespective of any objections the insurer may have against the insured arising from the insurance contract which could release the former from the obligation to pay the insurance money.

The Greek law on MTPL requires insurance coverage of the civil liability of the driver, the owner or the car's possessor in case of a motor accident, in its entirety. Self-evidently, it does not increase the extent of the liable persons' civil liability. In line with the principles of underwriting, MTPL coverage does not encompass any share of liability which exceeds the minimum insured amount.

244. If the motor vehicle is likely to be exposed to special risks of civil liability, such as races and contests of speed, precision or skill, insurance must include such special risks while a special insurance certificate is issued thereto.

Coverage is also indirectly confined by the meaning of the term 'third party'. The following persons are excluded from the notion of 'third party': the driver of the vehicle causing the damage, any other person whose liability is covered by the policy, the party contracting with the insurer and the legal representatives of a juridical person or of a commercial company which is not a legal person, when these persons are insured.

245. As mentioned, the MTPL insurer cannot invoke any objections arising out of the policy against the injured third party, claiming against him by way of direct action. The insurer is, however, entitled to turn against the liable driver for recovery. Thus, exclusions from coverage provided in the general terms of MTPL insurance are valid only against the insured and not against the third party who has suffered the loss.

It is important to mention that the insurer is not allowed to insert exclusions from coverage in the policy except for the following three ones, provided for by the law: (1) if the driver was not in possession of the driving licence; (2) if the driver was driving the car under the influence of alcohol or toxic substances, insofar driving under the influence of alcohol, etc., is causally linked with the accident. In case the driver was under the influence of alcohol or toxic substances and the car was rented by a rent-a-car enterprise, the MTPL insurer has no recovery claim against the rent-a-car enterprise; (c) if the car was used for purposes different than those provided by its official registration certificate. However, the insurer cannot effectively invoke these exclusions from his liability against the claimant/injured party; once the insurer pays the indemnity to the latter, he has the right to turn against the liable driver and, as the case may be, against the owner or the person in possession of the car, in case such persons are other than the driver.

II. Persons Obliged to Conclude the Insurance

246. The owner or the person in possession of the vehicle is the person obliged to conclude insurance covering the risk of civil liability arising from damages incurred by third parties, including passengers of the car, arising out of motor accidents. The term 'motor vehicles', within the meaning of the law, denotes vehicles moving on the ground, propelled by mechanical power or by electricity, regardless of the number of their wheels. It does not cover vehicles which are moving on rails other than trams. Trailers, whether coupled to the motor vehicle or not, and bicycles propelled by an auxiliary motor, are regarded as motor vehicles. Case law does not consider it necessary for the car to be in motion at the moment the loss occurred.

247. Automobiles belonging to the state and (on condition of reciprocity) to foreign states are exempted from compulsory insurance, as are automobiles belonging to intergovernmental organizations. All automobiles belonging to these categories must be equipped with a document, issued from the competent authority, certifying their status. In the case of automobiles belonging to foreign states or intergovernmental organizations, the certificate must specify the Authority or organization liable to pay the insurance money and which may, therefore, be sued before courts.

If the damage is caused by a person making unauthorized use of a motor vehicle belonging to a person exempted from compulsory insurance, the exempted person bears the same limited liability towards the injured third party as the 'Auxiliary Fund for the Insurance of Liability Arising from Motor Accidents'.

248. The persons who are obliged to take up coverage but fail to do so and who run the motor vehicle or allow it to be run by another person are liable to a fine of up to EUR 500 and a penalty payment of up to EUR 3,000. Drivers also may face other sanctions, such as licence-plate removal and the withdrawal of their driver's licence.

III. The Insurer Who Provides Compulsory Motor Vehicle Liability Insurance

249. Compulsory motor vehicle liability insurance is concluded with insurers authorized by law to conclude motor vehicle liability insurance, provided they are members of the Association of Greek Insurance Companies. The Association is required by law to admit as its members all insurance companies which are lawfully conducting motor vehicle liability insurance.

If coverage cannot be obtained, the interested party applies to a permanent special pricing committee which sets the premium and terms of cover to be provided. By virtue of an application, the interested party seeks insurance cover from the insurance company of its choice, notifying it that the premium-determining process has been set. The insurer is bound thereafter to provide insurance cover from the date on which the application for insurance cover was filed with it. At the same time, the law provides that the insurer is not entitled to refuse to conclude or renew an insurance contract without specific reasons justifying his refusal. Breach of this obligation may entail monetary sanctions.

IV. Proof of Insurance Coverage

250. It is prohibited for all motor vehicles to be driven without the coverage of the respective insurance.

The existence of insurance coverage is certified by a written document issued by the insurer stating the period of insurance. This certificate should be always carried in the motor vehicle.

251. A motor vehicle with foreign registration plates is considered to be insured if it bears a valid policy certificate issued in its country. However, if this country is not member of the Unified Agreement signed in Rethymno (Greece) on 30 May 2002, the said motor vehicle must be equipped with a Green Card (international insurance certificate) issued by a motor insurance bureau which has signed an agreement with the Greek International Insurance Bureau (*see* paragraph 259) for the settlement of claims arising from accidents occurring abroad.

Motor vehicles bearing registration plates of another EEA country are not subject to compulsory control as to the existence of MTPL coverage when entering Greece, but still random control is possible.

252. If the motor vehicle is duly insured, it cannot become the object of precautionary seizure for the satisfaction of claims arising from accidents caused by its circulation, in case the accident has caused personal injuries, except for circumstances where the claim exceeds the insured amount. In this case, the vehicle may be seized for the excess amount. If an accident occurs, the driver must produce and present a copy of the insurance certificate in order to be released from the precautionary seizure.

V. Transfer of the Insurance Coverage

253. The cancellation, expiry or suspension of the insurance contract may be invoked as a defence against the injured party only in case the accident occurs after sixteen days have elapsed since the insurer notified the insured or the contracting party of such cancellation, expiry or suspension. The relevant notice must be tendered in writing at the insured's or the contracting party's domicile or place of residence.

254. In the event of the owner's death, his rights and obligations under the insurance policy are transferred to the person inheriting the motor vehicle, unless the new owner notifies the insurer within a month from the death that he does not accept such rights and obligations.

VI. Insurance Contract Relations and Direct Action (Action Dirécte)

255. Article 9 of Codified Law 489/1976 (Greek MTPL Act) is one of the few provisions contained in this piece of legislation bearing 'insurance contract law' nature providing as it provides that the insured or the contracting party is bound to report to the insurer, within eight working days at the latest, any accident concerning the insured vehicle of which he has obtained knowledge. The insured or the contracting party must also provide the insurer, upon the insurer's request, with all necessary information or documents, as well as all necessary legal assistance. The insured has the further obligation to provide the insurer with all information and documents provided by the insurance policy. Breach of the above obligations gives rise to the obligation to compensate the insurer for any loss caused thereby. Further rules of the same nature are these contained in Article 6 b, which provides the three *ex lege* exclusions from coverage (*see* paragraph 245) and Article 6 c, which obliges the insurer to provide to the insured, upon the latter's request, a certificate depicting any sums of insurance money paid to injured third parties for the period such person has been insured by the insurer granting the certificate.

256. The injured party has an independent claim against the insurer under the insurance contract up to the insured sum (action dirécte). Where more than one person is injured, and the total indemnity requested exceeds the insured sum, each individual claim is proportionally reduced so that the injured parties are satisfied according to the extent of their loss. If an injured party receives a sum in excess of his proportionate share due to the insurer's ignorance as to the existence of other claims or in execution of a court judgment, the insurer is liable towards the remaining injured parties only up to remainder of the insurable sum. These parties have a right of recovery from the party who received the excess amount.

The action dirécte may not apply as to the extent of liability which exceeds the obligatory minimum insurable amount, provided that there is a relevant provision thereto in the policy.

VII. The 'Auxiliary Fund'

257. The MTPL Act provides for the establishment of the 'Auxiliary Fund for the Insurance of Liability Arising from Motor Accidents'.

All insurance undertakings writing motor vehicle insurance are obligatorily members of the Auxiliary Fund.

258. The Auxiliary Fund is obliged to indemnify the injured party only for death, bodily injury or material losses, in the following circumstances:

(i) where the party liable for the accident is unidentified;
(ii) where the vehicle at fault was uninsured;
(iii) where the accident was caused by a vehicle of special type bearing special registration plates, the liability of its driver, either owner or possessor, not being covered by MTPL insurance;
(iv) if the insurer was declared insolvent or if the execution of a judgment against it has been proven fruitless or if it has had its licence withdrawn due to breaches of the law. The liability of the Auxiliary Fund is subsidiary to the liability of the driver/owner and its MTPL insurer. Thus, the injured party must have no other means at his disposal for compensation by an insurer other than the Fund.

VIII. The International Insurance Bureau (Green Card Bureau or Motor Insurers' Bureau)

259. The Bureau is a private law corporation, as is the Auxiliary Fund.

The aim of the Bureau is to: (a) indemnify victims of accidents caused in Greece by a motor vehicle usually stationed outside Greece, and (b) indemnify victims of accidents occurring abroad caused by motor vehicles usually stationed in Greece.

260. All insurance companies performing MTPL insurance services in Greece are obligatorily members of the Bureau.

The Bureau delivers international insurance certificates (Green Cards) to its members and its members issue such to persons intending to travel to or through countries where Green Card coverage is required.

IX. Frontier Insurance

261. Motor vehicles entering Greece which are not insured as required by the law on third-party motor liability insurance and are not in possession of a Green Card are obliged to obtain coverage by special insurance upon entering the Greek territory (frontier insurance). Coverage must have a minimum duration of thirty days and cannot be renewed. Such frontier insurance is carried out by the International Insurance Bureau which has offices established at the Greek frontier stations for this purpose. Such motor vehicles may, of course, be covered by regular insurance as well.

Chapter 2. The Mandatory General Terms of Motor Vehicle Liability Insurance

§1. General Remarks

262. It has already been mentioned that no uniform policy is followed in formulating general insurance conditions in Greece; rather, each insurance enterprise specifies its own general terms. The general conditions of motor vehicle insurance are not anymore an exception. In the past, the law had arranged for conformity in general terms determining them by way of a Ministerial Decision, which was in force between 1978 and 2007. This unusual practice was justifiable, though, given the compulsory nature of this insurance, which necessitates the strict control of its terms. In spite of the abolishment of the compulsory use of the above-mentioned general insurance terms, the insurance industry still uses, to a great extent, these rules on a voluntary basis. An important difference associated with the abolishment of the aforesaid Ministerial Decision and the incorporation of some of its provisions in the MTPL Act concerns the chapter on exclusions from coverage: while the original relevant term, embodied in the Ministerial Decision, included twenty-five exclusions, the new statutory law confines those exclusions to three, as mentioned above. Thus, given the similarity of the previous and the standing legislation on this issue, the value of the relevant existing Greek case law is still apparent.

263. Apart from the above general terms, there are other optional terms for 'own damage', fire and theft insurance. These are further examined in paragraphs 277 et seq. on motor vehicle (non-liability) insurance.

264. The general terms of motor insurance consist of three parts: the first section concerns the general provisions, the second section concerns civil liability insurance and the third part contains limitations and exclusions from coverage.

§2. General Provisions

I. Compulsory and Optional Terms

265. The general provisions of the general conditions of motor accident liability insurance are important not only as to the coverage of the risk of the driver's liability but also as to the coverage of the risks of 'own damage', fire and theft. The application of the above general provisions to motor vehicle own damage, fire and theft coverage is optional, as this application is provided in the 'general insurance conditions against own damage, etc.', which are uniform in view of their voluntary application as required by Insurance Associations for all insurance companies operating in Greece.

II. The Insurance Policy and Insurance Coverage

266. The parties may agree to provisional coverage prior to the issuance of the insurance policy, evidenced by a provisional memorandum of cover.

267. The insurance contract must specify, among others, the name and address of the insured, the owner and/or person in possession of the vehicle, the date of commencement and the duration of coverage, the vehicle's registration number, any other elements required for the calculation of the premium, the risks covered and the corresponding insured sums and the premium.

Any modification of these particulars is valid only if it takes place in writing and the contracting party is notified thereto.

III. Renewal and Suspension of Coverage and Notice of Cancellation

268. The insurance contract is valid for the period stated in the policy and is renewed for an equal period on expiry unless either contracting party notifies its counterparty to the contrary, thirty days before the contract's expiry. The law does not limit the duration of such contracts in the sense that no *ex lege* maximum duration is provided. Under the abolished compulsory insurance tariffs, it was required that MTPL insurance contracts must have a minimum duration of one month and a maximum duration of one year, being tacitly renewable.

Each renewal is accompanied by the issuance of a Renewal Certificate.

269. The insurance contract may be suspended at the written request of the policyholder. Suspension commences twenty days after the insurer receives the request. If a suspension is granted for an indefinite period, the insurance contract becomes effective again following a written request from the policyholder thereto. If the suspension has been granted for a definite period, the period of insurance is extended for a period equal to that of the suspension, or the premium corresponding to the period of suspension is refunded.

It may be agreed in writing that during the period of suspension, cover against the risks of fire and other risks remain in force under certain conditions.

270. The insured is entitled, at any time, to give notice of cancellation of the contract by registered mail. The insurer, instead, cannot cancel the contract unless there is a special serious reason for that. The cancellation becomes effective after thirty days have elapsed from service of the insurer's notice. This does not contradict the fact, mentioned above (paragraph 253), that termination of the insurance contract becomes effective sixteen days after notification because the former provision concerns the relations between the insurer and insured, whereas the latter concerns the relations between the insurer and third parties.

Prepaid premiums are refundable in the case of cancellation.

IV. Changes in Ownership or Possession of the Motor Vehicle

271. In the event of change in the ownership or possession of the motor vehicle, the insurance contract is terminated *ipso jure* after the lapse of thirty days unless, within the same period, the original policyholder or the new owner or the new possessor asks for coverage to be continued and the insurer does not reject such request within ten days. The insurer is not liable vis-à-vis the insured for payment of insurance money if a new insurance contract has been concluded after the above change in ownership or in possession relating to the same motor vehicle.

V. Contractual Obligations

272. The compliance of the insured and the policyholder with the policy terms is a prerequisite for the insurer's liability. As said, only in three cases where there is an *ex lege* exclusion from coverage the insurer can recover against the insured the amount of the indemnity paid to the injured party. Under the previous law which provided that the Auxiliary Fund was also burdened with the duty to compensate the third injured party if the car accident was intentionally caused, the insurer was not liable vis-à-vis the injured party but only against the Auxiliary Fund, which in turn had a respective recovery claim against the insured driver. As regards the breach of the insured's obligation to notify the claim to the insurer and collaborate with him, the latter has only a claim for indemnity against the insured, unless the insured has intentionally omitted to notify the insurer.

General provisions on insurance contract law, contained in the ICA, are applicable in motor liability insurance if the wording of the provisions of the special law (MTPL Act) or its spirit is not violated. The applicant of insurance must disclose to the insurer the particulars of the risk and all related information requested on facts or events likely to affect the assessment of the risk.

During the period of coverage, the policyholder must promptly inform the insurer of any change in the particulars referred above or of any circumstances likely to variate or aggravate the risk, as well as of any change in the ownership or the possession of the vehicle.

Non-compliance with the above obligations attributed to fraud of the applicant entitles the insurer to avoid coverage. In the case of gross negligence, the insurer's obligation to pay the insurance money can only be reduced. There have not been reported cases where the insurer has paid the insurance money to the victim of a car accident and, in turn, exercised his recovery right against the insured who has breached these obligations. Greek law does not exclude this possibility.

273. Upon the occurrence of the peril, both the ICA and the MTPL Act provide that the policyholder is obliged to inform the insurer promptly and to proceed with all possible actions to minimize the loss and offer the insurer any reasonable assistance and necessary information thereto. The respective term of the policies sets out these obligations in detail.

The insured and the policyholder are liable for the restoration of any damages sustained by the insurer due to intentional breach of the aforesaid obligations.

Any acknowledgement of debt or admission of responsibility by the policyholder or the insured towards any third party who has suffered a loss as well as any agreement reached by them entailing increment of their liability are of no effect for the insurer unless made with his written consent. The policyholder and the insured are liable for the restoration of any loss suffered by the insurer because of their incorrect admission of liability or acknowledgement of debts.

§3. Civil Liability Insurance Provisions

274. An old clause common in motor insurance, which provides for that 90% of the insured amount refers to the maximum limit of the insurer's liability for indemnity and 10% to default interest, court and other expenses, has been declared invalid by the Courts. The Courts have considered that the insurer is, in principle, liable for court expenses, irrespectively of their amount. As far as the previously mentioned clause is concerned, if either of the above amounts is lower than the respective percentage, the insurer's liability extends up to the entire insured amount.

275. Liability relating to trailers may either be covered by the policy covering the towing vehicle or separately. In the first case, insurance of the trailer is only valid for the part exceeding the amount insured for the towing vehicle.

In the case of coverage by separate policies, insurance of the trailer is valid only as long as the towing vehicle is uninsured or its insurance does not cover the trailer.

Unless otherwise provided in the policy, the cover does not include liability for accidents caused by the trailer while used as a tool, but only for accidents caused by its circulation on roads.

276. By virtue of the policy, the policyholder and the insured grant the insurer an irrevocable power of attorney in the sense that the insurer, provided he does not deny his liability originating from the contract, may represent them before any court and Authority for the purpose of defending third-party claims against the policyholder or the insured. Thus, the insurer is entitled to proceed to an amicable settlement of any third-party claims against himself or against the insured. Such settlement shall not, however, be binding for the insured, who can dispute such liability if he wishes.

Chapter 3. Own Damage Fire and Theft Motor Vehicle Insurance

§1. General Remarks

277. Motor vehicle insurance for own material damage also includes the risks of fire and theft. This coverage is non-compulsory and is always granted by the insurer who covers third-party motor vehicle liability.

As mentioned above, this insurance is commonly governed by uniform or similar general terms.

One general exclusion from coverage is that the insurance does not cover wear and tear, reduced performance, reduction of commercial value or loss of use. In addition, as regards the risk of theft, the local market regularly uses a clause restricting coverage, according to which the insurer's obligation to pay insurance money up to the car's value does not commence before the lapse of a short time from the day the theft occurred, while the insurer does not provide insurance money for damages and/or losses, which constitute further/consequential losses arising from the theft, unless a special provision is included thereto and an additional premium has been paid.

§2. Coverage for Own Damages of the Car

278. According to the local market's common practice, own damages of the car are covered if they are caused exclusively by collision, impact, overturning and falling over of the car. As a rule, the insurance does not cover losses related to the vehicle's standard accessories and equipment; a special agreement is required for such coverage. Further, own damage is not covered in cases of unauthorized use of the vehicle, unless otherwise agreed.

If own damages' insurance has been agreed upon by a franchise clause for a given amount per accident, the insurer is liable only for losses in excess of the amount of the franchise. However, such franchise clause in liability insurance cannot be invoked against the injured party, and further, it is questionable whether such clauses, in particular, if the percentage is high, can be legally included in the contract because they can harm the insurer's solvency.

§3. Coverage for Fire of the Car

279. Fire insurance covers damage to the insured vehicle originating from fire or lightning. It also includes damage to the vehicle due to its explosion.

§4. Coverage for Theft of the Car

280. Theft insurance covers the actual value of the car on the day of its loss. The insurer's liability depends on whether the loss was declared without delay to the Police Authorities and to himself. The insurer's liability commences only ninety days after the date of the filing of a charge, on two conditions: the insurer must produce a certificate proving that the charge is not in suspense, and it must not otherwise result that the vehicle was found in the meantime. The insurer is liable to pay the insurance money if the vehicle is found after the lapse of the above period. The insured is not entitled to withdraw charges even after the insurance money has been paid; otherwise, he must compensate the insurer for any loss caused thereby.

Against payment of the insurance money, the insurer may ask the car's owner to grant the insurer a written authorization and an irrevocable power of attorney enabling him (the insurer) to sell the car when found and to retain the proceeds, if he so wishes. He may also ask for a preliminary notarial agreement to be signed, enabling the insurer to demand the signature of a final agreement for the transfer of the ownership of the recovered vehicle to himself or to any third person indicated by the insurer. The notarial agreement also grants the insurer the power to obtain ownership of the car by signing a notarial transfer of ownership himself.

If the vehicle is found before the day of payment, the insurer may refuse payment till a legal act is drawn up transferring ownership of the car to himself or to any third person he indicates.

If the vehicle is found after the insurance money has been paid, the policyholder or the insured owner is obliged to notify the insurer thereto as soon as he is informed of the fact.

Upon the insurer being informed that the vehicle has been found, he is bound to notify in writing the insured owner and ask him to state in writing, within two months, whether he wishes to keep the recovered vehicle and refund the insurance money he has received, plus interest and expenses. If the insured fails to reply within two months, he is deprived of the right ceded to him.

281. Partial theft insurance covers only damages occurring while the vehicle is stolen and arising from the removal of parts or accessories attached to the body of the vehicle which are indispensable for its operation, as well as own damages of the vehicle occurring during its unauthorized use.

§5. Obligations of the Parties

282. The insurer's obligation is confined to coverage of the current actual value of the vehicle or the insured parts or accessories which have been destroyed or stolen, up to the insured amount, including expenses of all kinds. The insurer is entitled, instead of monetary compensation, to undertake the repair of the vehicle. Otherwise, all rules of under-and-over-insurance are applicable.

§6. Claim Settlement

283. Disputes on the extent of the loss, but not as to the insurer's liability, are resolved by expert arbitration. Greek Civil Procedure Law provides that the arbitration document is ad solemnitatem (constitutional); thus, there is no arbitration agreement without a document. The insured must, therefore, sign the general terms containing the arbitration clause; otherwise, he is not bound by the arbitration agreement, as case law considers that the requirements for a valid arbitration agreement are the same as the ones for expert arbitration (*see* paragraph 40). Arbitration agreements with binding effect for this kind of insurance are not used in the Greek market.

§7. Limitations and Exceptions

284. Some usual exceptions and limitations of the coverage of own car damages which are applied in the local market, in addition to the exclusion of collision with other cars, are the following:

- damage to the vehicle as a result of inadequate maintenance;
- damage to the vehicle's tyres provided that it did not occur in conjunction with other damages for which coverage exists;
- in the absence of express agreement, damage to the vehicle's systems, such as refrigerators or heating appliances/chambers of cars;
- damage which occurred while the vehicle was travelling on roads not reserved for the circulation of vehicles or on roads on which authorities have forbidden traffic;
- damage caused directly or indirectly by acts of malice by persons instructed or inspired to take such actions by political organizations of any kind.

Part V. Insurance of the Person

Chapter 1. Workmen's Compensation and Occupational Disease

285. Workmen's compensation insurance is not extensively purchased by Greek employers. The reason for this is that the employers are obliged to be covered by social insurance, for workmen's accidents. If the employer is not in breach of this obligation, then the coverage by the social insurer replaces its civil liability.

Obligatory social insurance includes coverage for all accidents occurring at work and occupational diseases. In this way, workmen's compensation and occupational disease insurance are unnecessary for the employer since, even if the workman was entitled to greater compensation under the Civil Code, the claim would still be confined to the compensation payable under social insurance. This explains why the volume of this kind of insurance is low.

286. Workmen's private insurance coverage is, therefore, concluded on a voluntary basis by businessmen who choose to purchase such coverage for their personnel. Such coverage is complementary to social insurance. Whereas the Social Insurance Institution awards compensation in kind (medical care, etc.), workmen's compensation is agreed as a lump sum and is received in addition to the Social Insurance Institution's indemnity. Many undertakings voluntarily conclude group insurance covering workmen's compensation as a part of their corporate strategy. This insurance is concluded as a form of group insurance in favour of the employee, who, according to the specific wording of the policy, can obtain a direct right to claim the insurance money from the insurer. The insurer may claim the premium only from the employer, who is burdened with the duty to pay it. Albeit such insurance is concluded on a voluntary basis, if the employer offers such benefit continuously, the insurance money of such insurance is considered as part of the salary, unless differently provided. This insurance cover is concluded in addition to social insurance coverage, and the employer has a right to cumulative satisfaction of his claim. The existence of private insurance coverage does not, in any way, reduce the claim against the social insurer.

Two points need to be emphasized: first, the employer who has failed to take due measures for the coverage of his personnel by social insurance is fully liable to pay indemnity under civil law and on pain of criminal sanctions, in the event of a workman's death, illness or injury. The fact that he has voluntarily purchased private workmen's insurance does not restrict his liability. The employer also faces criminal sanctions for failing to pay all appropriate social security contributions. The employer may also be liable for criminal offences arising from the failure to provide a safe environment for its employees. As a matter of public policy, this liability cannot be covered by insurance. The second point is that case law considers the group insurance purchased by the employer, in principle, as part of wages, with the result that the employer has no right to restrict or cancel such coverage after he chooses to conclude it, as, under Greek labour law, employers are prohibited from restricting financial and institutionalized working conditions. If the employer proceeds to such cancellation or restriction unilaterally, the employee may claim the lost amount or, alternatively, take such action to be a cancellation of his contract with the employer and bring about the consequences provided by law.

If the worker changes employer, coverage does not terminate if the worker pays the premium corresponding to his individual coverage.

The aforementioned observations relate to group workmen's accident insurance on which there is no separate legislation, nor have insurers' associations specified general conditions for such group insurance, as every enterprise shapes individual conditions to its policies.

It is important to mention that the Social Insurance Institution does not cover moral damages claimed by workmen against the employer for accidents at work. Private insurance can provide coverage for this lacuna so that such coverage is the most popular in the relevant Greek market.

Chapter 2. Bodily Injuries Insurance

287. Insurance for bodily injuries may be concluded either as sum insurance (injuries' class of life insurance) or as indemnity insurance (*see* paragraph 123). Bodily injuries insurance is concluded as either coverage against a person's temporary or permanent disability for work or as coverage against the risk of death, resulting from an accident.

Coverage varies: when bodily injuries' insurance is concluded as sum insurance, the insurer may agree to pay a fixed sum if, for instance, the insured loses an arm, or to pay a daily allowance in the event of the insured's disability to work.

When written as indemnity insurance, the insurer's obligation relates to the insured's expenses for medical care, etc. It may also be agreed that a sum is paid in instalments for each day of the insured's continued disability and/or for each day of hospitalization.

Insurance against children's accidents, insurance against motor accidents (which is different from MTPL insurance), insurance against travellers', marine, bicycle and aeroplane accidents are all examples of this specific kind of insurance.

Chapter 3. Private Health Insurance

288. Insurance against illness covers the risk of deterioration of a person's health which did not result from an accident. It is concluded either as sum insurance, the payment of the insurance sum being effected in total or in instalments, or as indemnity insurance. The differentiation between deterioration of a person's health and a work-related accident is important for coverage. If it is proven that an illness is attributed to an earlier accident related to work, the loss shall be deemed as arising out of the accident, not as an independent illness. This issue is largely dealt with in the general conditions of coverage.

Private health insurance is becoming very popular recently because, despite extensive coverage of the respective risks by social insurance, the amount paid by social insurance is marginal and cannot embrace the expenses, especially those of hospitalization, which constantly and sharply increase, in particular because of the very expensive medical technology and medical equipment. Private health insurance can operate either supplementarily to or cumulatively with social insurance since 'over-insurance' is not prohibited in insurance of persons.

Chapter 4. Life Insurance

§1. General Remarks

289. The insurance of persons is not always concluded as sum insurance because, as mentioned above, the parties may choose to conclude such insurance under either the indemnity or the sum insurance system. An insurance enterprise active only in non-life insurance may also provide coverage for illness or bodily injuries under the indemnity system. It must be noted that the enterprise remains free to write such insurance as sum insurance as well. On the contrary, the non-life insurance enterprise cannot write life insurance.

In life insurance, the fixed sum insured matches the insurer's service. The sum payable does not depend on the existence or the extent of the loss. If a loss exists, the possibility that there is another liable party does not affect the extent of the insurer's obligation, nor does it give the insurer the right to be reimbursed by the liable party. The insured has a right to accumulate payments from more than one source.

290. The ICA contains no specific provisions on fixed sum insurance but only encompasses settings on indemnity insurance and life insurance. Consequently, the rules on indemnity insurance apply *mutatis mutandis* in cases where illness or injury coverage has been agreed upon under the indemnity system. The provisions on the insured's obligations, i.e., a pre-contractual obligation to disclose the risk and the obligation to inform the insurer of the changes of the risk during the life of the policy apply, but sanctions for their breach are imposed only in case of the insured's fraud. An obligation to promptly inform the insurer on the occurrence of the insured event is not further provided.

Unless the contrary has been agreed, life insurance covers death by suicide if death occurs more than two years after the conclusion of the contract or after an increase in the insured sum.

291. The obligation to pay the premium is regulated in the same way as in indemnity insurance. The rules that there is no insurance without advance payment of the premium and that the insurance contract may not be cancelled without prior notification apply here as well. The life-premium is differentiated, from the underwriting's viewpoint, into savings premium and risk premium. The savings element of life insurance premium obliges the life-insurer to offer the insured the option to 'buy out' the value of his coverage. This option is required by the ICA to be offered after the lapse of a maximum of three years, in view of the fact that the savings character of the premium is reinforced at this point of time. For group insurance policies, the period of three years is not binding for the insurer.

292. The general law institution of the 'contract for the benefit of a third party' applies to life insurance, as in other kinds of insurance, according to Greek law. This setting concerns cases where the policyholder concluded insurance against his own death and designated a third party as the beneficiary of the insurance money. The beneficiary is the third party for the benefit of whom the contract is concluded.

On the contrary, there is no 'contract for the benefit of a third party' in case the policyholder is also the person designated as the beneficiary of the insurance money within an insurance against the death of another person (!). In this case, the policyholder must have a lawful interest in concluding the insurance contract and must have obtained the written approval of the person at risk (e.g., the spouse concluding aviation insurance in the event of his wife's death whereby the beneficiary is the concluding party). Notably, the person at risk is regarded as the insured under Greek law, in cases of life insurance against the risk of death. Even if the right to appoint a beneficiary can be exercised, according to the contract, exclusively by the person at risk, the policyholder – in case he is other than the person at risk – cannot conclude such insurance without the written approval of the person at risk.

The beneficiary of the insurance money is either the insured (or his heirs in the case of death) or the person designated in the policy or in a separate written notification tendered to the insurer as the beneficiary or the assignee. If the party contracting with the insurer passes away, regardless of whether the insurance has been concluded on his/her own life or on the life of a third party, the beneficiary does not collect the insurance money in his capacity as a heir of the person at risk but in his capacity as beneficiary.

In addition, if the policyholder goes bankrupt, this has no effect on the rights of the beneficiary.

§2. Life Insurance

I. Term Life Insurance

293. From insurance contracts' point of view and pursuant to the principles governing such contracts, life insurance includes coverage of the risk of death and the risk of survival, which are commonly sold as a package, in conjunction with annuities' coverage. From a supervisory standpoint and in accordance with the classification of the licences granted to the insurer to conduct insurance business, life insurance may further include a combination of coverage against the risks of death, survival and annuities coupled with investments or in conjunction with accident or illness coverage as far as both are granted complementarily to the main coverage, i.e., the insurance against death, survival, annuities, as well as marriage and birth insurance.

Life insurance entails contracts including only a risk element and contracts combining risk and saving elements. The latter concerns long-term insurance and is the most popular. The premium payable in cases of the above-mentioned 'combined life insurance' constitutes a combination of a risk and a savings premium. A combination of a risk and savings premium is also apparent in the death insurance for life. Savings premium is a part of the premium which the insurer retains as a reserve (technical provision) to be returned to the insured in the future (capitalization insurance). The calculation of this reserve constitutes an internal procedure of the insurer, supervised by the Supervisor of Insurance. Every insurer who sells capitalization insurance, i.e., life insurance with a saving element, has to incorporate in the contract an annex stating the insurance money to be paid to the insured for each year in case the latter elects to exercise his right to demand the repurchase of the policy (surrender value). The ICA states that no policy can be agreed, providing that the policyholder may not surrender the policy for more than three years since its conclusion. No restrictions are provided for group life insurance.

Purely risk life insurance is agreed upon for a short term, usually to cover a special risky situation, such as the period of a voyage. It contains only a risk premium which is consumed every year in exchange of the undertaken risk. The market usually distributes such insurance in the form of group insurance, concluded by tour operators, banks, sports clubs, etc., in favour of their clients, in return for a low premium. The purely survival insurance is also a purely risk insurance and is extremely uncommon in the market.

Instead, long-term death insurance (for a period of, e.g., twenty or thirty years) coupled with survival insurance is popular in the Greek insurance market. In such insurance, the insurer is required either to pay the insured a fixed sum, if he survives the coverage period, or to effect payment to the beneficiaries specified, if the insurance risk, i.e., the insured's death, materialized during the coverage period. In such insurance, while the savings element is high and the element of risk is low at the beginning of coverage, the internal relationship of these elements is reversed over time. In long-term life insurance, distribution of the insurer's profits derived from successful investments of the earned premiums or a reduction of the payable premium after a certain period is usually agreed upon.

II. Annuities/Endowment

294. In annuities, the insured event occurs when the insured reaches a certain age which is stated in the contract. The insurer is obliged to effect payment of the insurance money either all at once or in monthly instalments, according to the terms of the policy, whereas if the insured dies, the insurer is released. The payment of instalments resembles a private pension. If instalments are provided, the insurer faces two uncertainties. The one concerns the possibility of the insured reaching the age stated in the contract, and the other relates to the number of instalments that will be paid until the insured's death. The second uncertainty may be partially addressed by way of imposition of a cap on the aggregate amount which the insurer will be obliged to pay.

III. Own-Life Insurance

295. Both term life insurance for death and survival and annuities insurance can be concluded either for the account of the policyholder or for the account of a third party. In own-life insurance, the policyholder is insured and is called the person at risk because the risk is directly related to events of his life. As insured, he is entitled to collect the insurance money unless he has designated one or more persons as beneficiaries. As said before (*see* paragraph 292), in death insurance, the beneficiaries are the heirs of the person at risk or the person(s) designated as beneficiary(ies).

IV. Insurance on the Life of a Third Person

296. While the stipulation of life insurance for the account of a person other than the policyholder falls under the institution of 'insurance for the account of another person' which covers all insurance, a special situation is apparent in the case of death insurance. As said above (paragraph 292), both: (a) death insurance whereby the policyholder is not the person at risk, whereby that person has granted the policyholder the right to designate a beneficiary; and (b) death insurance of the policyholder, whereby a third party is designated as the beneficiary, fall under general law's institution of 'contract for the benefit of a third party'. In the first case, the person at risk is the beneficiary because he/she has the right to appoint a beneficiary of the insurance money in case of his/her own death, but he/she also can claim the surrender value of the policy. In the second case, the beneficiary has the right to claim the insurance money in the case of death of the person at risk.

V. Other Cases of Life Insurance

297. In Greece, as a rule, purely life insurance (death or survival insurance or a combination of both) is sold packaged with other personal insurance, in particular with illness and annuities insurance. The purely life coverage concerns the so-called basic or main insurance in exchange of a fixed premium, entitling the insured to collection of a fixed insured sum. It is concluded as long-term insurance. Popular ancillary risks, accompanying such insurance, include hospitalization and of medical care in general. The premium of the latter is, as a rule, much higher than the premium of the main coverage because it covers the expenses of hospital care, which are high and permanently increasing.

The peculiarity of this type of insurance is that it concerns a combination of a long-term, fixed sum insurance (death, survival, a combination of both), with an indemnity insurance (medical care). Insurers conducting business in Greece seldom provide such medical care coverage for a period of only one year which can be renewed upon the insurer's discretion, the latter being free to properly adjust the payable premium. Instead, usually no duration is provided as to the coverage of this ancillary risk so that, in view of its ancillary nature to the long-term main coverage, it follows its same duration. This practice has caused a considerable number of disputes, in particular during the recent period of economic recession. Part of the aforesaid policies provides a formula for the adjustment of the premium of the medical care coverage, while another part, which comprises the policies issued in the 1990s, does not. In both cases, the Courts have adjudicated that the insurer has the right to adjust the amount of the premium during the long life of such insurance, but this adjustment has to be agreed upon bilaterally and not unilaterally. This requirement implies serious hindrances for insurers, given the lack of a collective mechanism provided for in the law that could be applied to ensure fair premiums.

Even in cases where an adjustment formula of the premium is provided in the policy, it is quite often judged that such formula is not valid as non-transparent or not clear enough, or because it constitutes a surprise to the insured, in the sense that it was impossible for him to apprehend, at the time of the contract's conclusion, the objective criteria on which any future increase of the premium would be based on.

298. Life insurance linked with investments (unit-linked) used to be very popular in the 1990s, where the index of the country's Stock Exchange increased ten times and continued to be a prosperous activity for insurers till the economic crisis that broke out in 2009. Unit-linked insurance is sold usually in conjunction with the main coverage (death, survival or a combination of both) and not coupled with coverage of the risks of annuities, marriage and birth. The law imposed on the insurer selling unit-linked products a number of obligations, concerning the provision of information to the insured and the Supervisor of Insurance, demanding extra qualifications of the persons-in-charge of unit-linked products' sales – the latter being almost identical to the obligations of investment products' distributors, although the investment element included in the unit-linked insurance is not that sophisticated and complicated. It is to be noted that Greek law does not introduce a limit as to the percentage that the insured risk must stand for in unit-linked insurance. Thus, it can be supported that the insurer can exercise the class of unit-linked life insurance as a pure investment company. However, those products are sold usually with some risk element to be better marketed as investment products, packaged with insurance.

Part VI. Private Insurance and Social Security

299. Traditionally, social insurance in Greece has taken up an important part of insurance business, normally conducted by private life-insurers. That is one of the reasons for the very low percentage of the premium per capita. Because of the crucial actuarial deficits of the social insurance institutions and the warnings that the pension is not any more secured, the private sector has penetrated to cover such gap. However, this trend has diminished because of the crisis of 2009. The largest social insurer has been the Social Insurance Institution offering general social insurance (*see* paragraph 133), which has been substituted by the EOPYY as far as social healthcare insurance is concerned and by the Single Social Security Entity (e-EFKA) as far as social pensions are concerned. Notably, legislation on the formation of EOPYY and e-EFKA contains only provisions of a rather administrative nature, purporting at the unification of the previously individual social insurance institutions, their liability being still regulated by the separate laws that established each of them. Until recently, almost every separate profession had its own social insurance organization for health and pension coverage, each of which provided for different solvency margins, contributions and quality of services and coverage. Successive governments have pledged to reform this vast and inefficient system, and recently, the compulsory merger of social insurance organizations into one took place, leading to the formulation of the two aforesaid entities (EOPYY and e-EFKA).

In Greece, social insurance is, in principle, an insurance of persons and, exceptionally, insurance against damages. There is no codified national law on social insurance as each of the previously independent social insurers is governed by separate rules. Regulations on Social Insurance Institution and some other social insurers provide a favourable regulation since they grant them the right of subrogation against a liable person for the accident of each insured, even before the social insurer has paid the social insurance money.

Social insurance derives from the law and not from a contract thereto and thus is obligatory. That is the main difference between private and social insurance. In private insurance, the insurance benefit is based on contract, even if such contract is not an insurance policy, but a collective agreement, where the insured is a member. *Ex lege* (social) insurance arises out of the employment relationship. The employer is obliged to notify his/her employees to the social insurer and is subject to sanctions if he fails to do so.

300. In Greece, it is prohibited for anyone whose work may be classified as falling within the scope of an 'employment relationship', to work without being socially insured. However, prior to the unification of the social insurance institutions, there were various professions (printers, merchants, pharmacists, doctors, attorneys, etc.) whose members were insured by social insurers other than Social Insurance Institution. In certain cases (e.g., for engineers who enter into a labour relationship with an employer), coverage by Social Insurance Institution remained compulsory and, thus, concurrent with the special coverage described above. The person insured by more than one social insurer was released from the obligation to pay premiums to Social Insurance Institution only if coverage by the other insurer(s) was as extensive as that of Social Insurance Institution. In other cases (e.g., attorneys), the possibility of concurrent liability of the Social Insurance Institution was excluded. All these issues have been largely surmounted since the unification of social insurance institutions.

301. A characteristic of social insurance is that the social insurer is a legal person of public law and, thus, is not obliged to maintain technical provisions covering the reimbursements it may be requested to pay, contrary to private insurance undertakings. The fact that social insurance is provided by public law entities generates state's responsibility for its proper function.

302. As regards the relationship of the insurer and the insured, the rules of overinsurance, underinsurance, subrogation, etc., do not apply in social insurance. Disputes between the social insurer and the insured are of public law nature and are resolved before administrative courts.

The provisions on Social Insurance Institution's liability are the most detailed among the regulations establishing the liability of the previously individual social insurance institutions. As mentioned, in MTPL insurance, the claim of the insured by Social Insurance Institution for collection of indemnity for bodily injuries against the tortfeasor is directly transferred to Social Insurance Institution *ex lege*, from the time the accident occurs, irrespectively of the time the insurer pays the insurance money.

Part VII. Insurance Intermediaries

Chapter 1. Law of Establishment and Supervision

§1. General Remarks

303. Private insurance business is carried out with the help of individuals or legal entities who act as insurance intermediaries. There are three kinds of insurance intermediaries in Greece: the insurance agent, the insurance broker and the coordinator of insurance agents.

Another kind of insurance intermediary is the so-called ancillary insurance intermediary (AII), which has been introduced by Law 4583/2018 that harmonized EU Directive 2016/97 on insurance distribution (IDD). AIIs resemble, as far as their role and activities are concerned, the so-called tight intermediaries of the previous legislation. AIIs have limited power in providing intermediary services, insofar their activities are provided as a supplement to their main business, which does not relate to insurance (e.g., a travel agency that offers its clients travel insurance as a supplement to its main service, i.e., the organization and execution of a travel). Albeit the provision of supplementary insurance services is widespread in the banking sector, banks cannot offer such services under the capacity of an AII. Instead, banks offering such services to their clients are obliged to enrol in the (special) Registry of Insurance Intermediaries as insurance agents. It should be noted that the bank's main privilege, when involved in the distribution of insurance products, is their clients' confidence, in contrast to the insurers and the common intermediaries. In this way, banks sell complicated investment products packaged as insurance, which a common intermediary would not always be able to sale. Banks are bound by bank assurance agreements concluded with the insurers, while some banks conclude such agreements with more than one insurer.

A smaller portion of AIIs' activities involves insurance business conducted by big stores, selling equipment and devices to consumers in combination with insurance, related to the products they sell.

304. The majority of intermediaries in Greece have been enrolled in the relevant Intermediaries' Registry under the capacities of insurance agent and insurance consultant – a category of the previous law that has been abolished, all the persons enrolled under this capacity being automatically transferred into the category of insurance agents. The services offered by these intermediaries are of a consulting nature. It is also notable that the employees of insurance companies may also act as salesmen on a commission basis, upon the discretion of the insurance company. In that regard, the employees of insurance companies, who are involved with the sale of insurance products and, in general, contact customers, as well as the respective employees of insurance intermediary undertakings, have to be qualified and certified in order to execute their business lawfully.

305. Loss surveyors, as well as loss adjusters, are persons with specific technical expertise who are freelance professionals, sometimes working at an international level, employed by insurance and reinsurance companies for the valuation of damages covered by insurance.

The surveyor appointed by an insurance company for the estimation of losses is obliged to submit a copy of his survey to the insured who suffered the loss, and the insurance company must notify the insured as to whether it accepts the survey. Such acceptance obliges the company to pay the insurance money. If it fails to pay after having accepted the survey, its licence may be withdrawn.

Surveyors' reports constitute cogent evidence but are not binding for the Courts. The law does not specify the conditions precedent for a person to become a surveyor. Many surveyors operate according to international standards, especially in the field of maritime risks.

There also exists a Body of Sworn Surveyors which performs surveys of the insured's property before and after the loss occurs.

306. Apart from the above-mentioned categories of insurance intermediaries whose function is recognized by law, the legal representative (mentioned in paragraph 67) of foreign insurance companies operating in Greece could, under the previous legislation, act as an intermediary for the company he represented. The legal representative is an instrument of the company whose existence is a prerequisite for the establishment of any non-Greek insurance company. The legislation governs the representative's duties and liability towards the state and third parties, while the company remains free to regulate further its own relations with the representative. Under the previous legal framework, the legal representative was entitled to maintain a personal clientele, except if otherwise provided in his contract, which he placed with the company, as is the case with insurance agents. This practice was indeed quite widespread. Commission payable for such placement differed from the commission payable to other intermediaries but was determined independently. Thus, the legal representative could also be an intermediary, but his activities as an intermediary were not supervised by the state. In other words, he was an insurance intermediary from an economic and not from a legal point of view.

Finally, an insurance company may also act as an intermediary from an economic point of view, between another insurer and the insured. For instance, under certain circumstances, a company with a highly developed network may proceed to portfolio placements with another insurer active in insurance classes in which the former is not himself active.

§2. LAW OF ESTABLISHMENT

307. Insurance agents, brokers and coordinators of insurance agents can be established in the country as either natural or legal persons. As natural persons, they can be freely established in any part of Greece, but they must be registered in the competent registry for insurance intermediaries. In order to be eligible as an insurance intermediary, the candidate must fulfil the requirements provided in the law which include, among others, compliance with education standards, a clean criminal record and compulsory professional liability insurance, while the exact extent of requirements slightly varies between insurance intermediaries and AIIs. The Regulator organizes examinations for the intermediary candidates at regular times.

Greece, like the other EU countries, has introduced the European passport for insurance intermediaries, meaning that the registration in the competent registry in one EU Member State grants the right to the intermediary to operate in Greece. A special record for non-Greek intermediaries is kept by the Bank of Greece. The prerequisites for the provision of (re)insurance services in Greece from distributors established in third countries (i.e., countries which are not numbered among those of the EEA) are differentiated between insurance undertakings and insurance intermediaries. Hence, on the one hand, insurance undertakings established in a non-EEA country, aiming to operate in Greece, have to acquire a relevant licence granted by the Bank of Greece under the condition of reciprocity and upon fulfilment of certain requirements, including the establishment of a branch, the appointment of a legal representative in Greece and compliance with the provisions on the Minimum Capital Requirement requested for insurance undertakings operating in Greece (Article 123 of Law 4364/2016). On the other hand, insurance intermediaries (physical persons or companies), which operate in a third country, need to follow the procedure required for intermediaries established in Greece; namely, they have to enrol in the Special Registry (of insurance products' distributors) by adducing the same documentation required for intermediaries established in Greece (Article 3 paragraph 4 of Law 4583/2018).

For EU citizens, the state may not impede establishment for reasons of public or market policy.

Furthermore, there are special provisions, regulating the freedom of services (FoS) regime for insurance intermediaries established in another EEA country, wishing to operate in Greece. The general concept is that insurance intermediaries are allowed to operate in any EEA Member State, given that they have already notified the competent supervisory authorities of their home, as well as of their host Member State. Thus, it can be inferred that there are no barriers to such cross-border activity within the EU, unless the intermediary is not registered in any EU registry.

Notably, intermediaries in the shipping industry operate from time to time via an establishment in the so-called offshore jurisdiction, mainly for taxation reasons, but also to avoid the extensive supervision provided for by EU legislation. A special regulation exists to facilitate entities, operating, among others, in ship management, ownership of ocean-going vessels, including insurance intermediation via an establishment in the country, with its headquarters in an offshore, third country.

§3. Law of Supervision

308. The activities of intermediaries are of public interest; their adherence to insurance legislation is, therefore, controlled by the Supervisor of Insurance who presides over the competent division of the Bank of Greece.

If the insurance agent, the broker, the coordinator of insurance agents or the AII infringes insurance legislation, the sanction may extend to the expulsion of the intermediary from the registry. Sanctions of penal nature against the insurance company and/or the insurance intermediary, as the case may be, are also provided.

Chapter 2. Insurance Intermediaries and the Insurance Contract

§1. Insurance Agents

309. The insurance agent, whether a natural or legal person, conducts business by virtue of a contract concluded with one or more insurance undertakings. He always has the capacity of a merchant. His activities include the presentation, preparation, pre-contractual arrangements and conclusion of contracts in the name and on behalf of the insurer. Furthermore, he is obliged to offer the insured his assistance/service, mainly of a consulting nature, regarding performance under the insurance contract, in particular, if the insured event occurs.

310. The rights and obligations of the insurance agent are described in a written agreement concluded between the insurer and the agent (agency agreement). Before its last amendment, legislation on insurance intermediaries (that was repealed and replaced by Law 4583/18) included certain provisions on this agency agreement. More especially: (i) the agency agreement had to be in written form, (ii) it was obligatory to be deposited to the Supervisor to be valid, (iii) without such an agreement no rights or obligations could arise for the parties and only general law could provide for some solutions in such circumstances, and (iv) sanctions were provided against the insurer and the agent who cooperated without having concluded an agency agreement.

The insurance agent may, according to the agreement, be employed by one insurance company exclusively or by more than one company. It is common, though, that the insurance agent works, in fact, as an insurance broker and vice versa. This is the case when the insurance agent has his own permanent clientele, so that, in case he has important clients/risks, he looks for the best (for him and the client) solution, even by writing the risk with an insurer other than the one with whom he has concluded the agency agreement. Thus, in case the agent has found a bilaterally more rewarding solution with a third insurer, he concludes an agency agreement ad hoc in order to place the important risk/client with him. To be noted that the agent is protected vis-à-vis the insurer, and this is not the case with the broker.

311. Agents' fees are usually arranged on a commission basis, which, in practice, usually ranges from 8% to 32.5% of net premiums. In life insurance, they may reach an even higher percentage for the first year, diminishing thereafter. However, it is not unusual for an insurance agent to be remunerated through the insurer's payroll or through a combined system of a commission and a salary. The manner of agents' remuneration does not affect their legal position, as the issue of their payment is regulated neither by the IDD nor by the Greek law 4583/2018 on insurance distribution.

312. The capacity of the manager or representative of an insurance undertaking operating in Greece is incompatible with the capacity of the insurance agent. In addition, the capacity of an insurance agent is incompatible with that of the insurance broker.

313. If the insurance agent's contract is terminated by the insurer for whichever reason, the latter is obliged to pay the agent a sum equating to the three years' commission that the agent would be entitled to receive if the agency agreement had not been terminated. The prerequisite for such payment is that the agent's clientele remains with the insurer. Hence, the commission to be paid to the agent represents only the value of the latter's clientele, which remains to the insurer and has not the nature of an indemnity for the contract's cancellation. However, if criminal proceedings against the agent, concerning offences emanating from his relationship with the insurer, are instituted, the payable sum is reduced to half. Nevertheless, in case of irrevocable acquittal of the agent, the insurer is obliged to pay the agent the remaining sum.

Under the preceding legal framework, the agent could not provide his services throughout the country. The related rule was introduced for the protection of free competition. This restriction has been abolished. Moreover, the foregoing law was interpreted as allowing the agent to engage in insurance activities which could not be strictly classified by law as services normally performed by agents, provided that these did not fall within the scope of activities belonging to other professions. Under the new law on distribution of insurance products, such interpretation is rather unnecessary as the law does not confine agents' business to certain activities.

§2. Insurance Brokers

314. Insurance brokers act on behalf of the insured and may not have any connection with a specific insurance company. However, their function as representatives of the insured's interests does not necessarily cover the entirety of the parties' relationship, which extends during the whole life of an insurance policy. Furthermore, even though brokers act independently from the individual insurer with whom they underwrite the risk in question, they commonly maintain framework agreements with several insurers, regulating their potential cooperation. These agreements are not regulated by the law, but they cannot be regarded as agency agreements and cannot change the capacity of the insurance broker. The Supervisory Authority, i.e., the Bank of Greece, collects data on the contracts brokers have concluded each year to ensure that they are acting independently. In practice, though, usually brokers are dependent on certain insurance companies, but this reliance is not disclosed to the insured. In the latter case, brokers can be characterized as 'pseudo-brokers', and their conduct can generate legal consequences, but this only rarely happens in Greece, as brokers' reliance on a certain insurance undertaking is usually kept secret. Finally, it must be noted that brokers have to be registered in the registry.

The brokers' clients who have taken out insurance have a priority lien over this security which precedes other general or special liens.

§3. Insurance Consultants [subagents and sub-brokers]

315. As stated above, the preceding legal framework on insurance mediation provided for another category of insurance intermediaries that have been abolished by the recent Law 4583/2018; they were called insurance consultants. Insurance consultants worked on behalf of one or more insurance companies or insurance agencies or insurance brokers, based on a written agreement. The consultants did not have the right to sign the insurance contract. Consultants were obliged to be registered in the competent registry and meet certain requirements (absence of a conviction for a criminal offence, higher education certificate, etc.). Consultants were merchants and were legally protected upon the termination of their contract with the insurance company in the same way as insurance agents since they were working on a commission basis. The object of the consultants' business was defined by law and corresponded to the so-called insurance subagent, a familiar institution in many European countries. The main tasks of the pre-existing insurance consultants are nowadays carried out by subagents and sub-brokers who work under the instructions of insurance agents or insurance brokers as their agents.

§4. Insurance Employees

316. Insurance employees, while not intermediaries themselves, are usually treated, in practice, as such in matters of remuneration: apart from standard wages, they can also receive a commission, following a relevant extra arrangement with the employer/insurer. This commission is payable even if the client approaches the employee simply by virtue of the latter's position as an employee and not through the employee's own initiative. Nevertheless, the commission is not considered as part of the employee's salary and, therefore, is not taken into account for the calculation of the compensation payable to the employee in case of termination of the employment relationship contract.

Part VIII. Reinsurance, Co-insurance, Pooling

Chapter 1. Reinsurance

317. The ICA provisions on the insurance contract and the provisions of the CPML on marine insurance contracts apply only *mutatis mutandis* in reinsurance contracts. There is no explicit provision in these acts, prohibiting their application to reinsurance contracts. In the very few relevant cases considered by the Greek Courts, it was held that the prescription period regarding the insured's claim against the insurer could not apply by way of analogy to claims of direct insurers against their reinsurers.

The extent of the application by analogy of these provisions has not been determined by case law because Greek Courts have dealt on only a few occasions with disputes between direct insurers and reinsurers. The fact that reinsurance contracts usually contain an arbitration clause is not the main reason for the lack of relevant case law; the main reason for such absence is the resolution of such disputes on an extrajudicial, commercial basis. It may be assumed that if there were an arbitration authority expressly competent for resolving such disputes, there would be a larger volume of case law on reinsurance.

318. The insured does not acquire rights vis-à-vis the reinsurer directly from the contract concluded by his direct insurer, nor does the insured acquire the right to obtain control over matters pertaining to the validity of such contract or a right of direct action against his first insurer's reinsurer. However, the insured is entitled to file a lawsuit against the reinsurer, only if the claim contained therein is the judicial recognition of the reinsurer's obligation to pay the reinsurance money to the direct insurer, who has covered the claimant. This can happen, in particular, in cases of fronting insurance where the direct insurer has transferred all the risk to the reinsurer.

The guarantees that the law requires to be tendered by the direct insurer are sufficient to safeguard the insured's interests, thus rendering the latter's further involvement in the reinsurance contract superfluous and leaving the matter in the hands of the direct insurer.

The opposite is, however, not the case: the reinsurer may intervene in the direct insurer's affairs and require him/her to control the loss if there is a special agreement in the reinsurance contract to that effect ('loss control clause'). In the absence of such clause, the reinsurer may not interfere in the direct insurer's handling of claims because the reinsurance contract is considered to contain an authorization to the direct insurer to handle the claims according to his own judgment, following the principle of utmost good faith. Notwithstanding, the reinsurer reserves a right, arising from general civil law provisions, to intervene in a contract's operation in cases of fraud committed by the direct insurer or if the direct insurer is in breach of good faith principles or business usages.

The insured's interest becomes more acute in cases of serious industrial risks covered by small direct insurers and almost entirely covered by reinsurance. Exact matching of the risk covered by the direct insurer with the risk covered by the reinsurer operates to the insured's advantage. To this effect, the insured may demand that the insurance contract contains a clause referring to the reinsurance contract.

319. Reinsurance is largely conducted in cases of risks undertaken by first insurers operating in the Greek market and is undertaken not only by reinsurers but also by direct insurers. However, reinsurance business is, to a great extent, written by reinsurers, and mostly large reinsurance undertakings which are based outside the country since, until today, there is no reinsurance undertaking licensed in Greece.

State control on reinsurance undertakings was introduced by the previously standing EU Reinsurance Directive, the provisions of which have been absorbed by the Solvency II Directive. State control over reinsurance undertakings is confined to the legitimacy of the reinsurer's activities and to the evaluation of reinsurance contracts' authenticity.

320. In the Greek reinsurance market, as in non-Greek markets, reinsurance falls under two basic categories: obligatory and facultative reinsurance. The parties to facultative reinsurance are free to choose the part of the risk to be covered. Facultative reinsurance includes contracts similar to those concluded under obligatory reinsurance, with the difference that they cover a specific risk of the direct insurer. Facultative reinsurance contracts are concluded to cover risks which are of such magnitude that cannot be covered in their entirety by obligatory reinsurance. The reinsurance conditions are usually agreed upon by a simple reference to the conditions applicable to the direct insurance contract. On the contrary, obligatory reinsurance is concluded for only a part of the direct insurer's entire business. The direct insurer, like his insured, is obliged to assign the risks to the reinsurer, who is obliged to accept them. This form of reinsurance is bilaterally obligatory, whereas in unilaterally obligatory reinsurance, called 'facultative-obligatory' reinsurance, the direct insurer may assign the risks at his discretion, and the reinsurer is obliged to accept such assignment.

321. Obligatory reinsurance is the most common type of reinsurance and can be divided into 'quota-share' reinsurance, 'excess capital' reinsurance and 'excess of loss' reinsurance. 'Quota-share' reinsurance coverage concerns a percentage of all or of a group of the direct insurer's risks. In 'excess capital' reinsurance, the reinsurer covers those parts of the risks which exceed the part retained by the direct insurer, while in 'excess of loss' reinsurance, the direct insurer's liability is restricted through the limitation of not the capital but the loss (non-proportionate reinsurance). These contracts may be concluded not only for each individual peril but also for classes of loss.

Reinsurance contracts are usually concluded for one year.

Chapter 2. Co-insurance and Pooling

322. Co-insurance is widely written in Greece since large risks, apart from being covered by reinsurance, are also distributed in the direct insurance market. However, the fact that co-insurance is common is attributed not only to underwriting policies but also to other reasons. For instance, a bank having an economic relationship with an insurance enterprise may persuade its (the bank's) clients to purchase insurance from the bank, while the client himself has a contractual relationship with another insurance company, or the same client may be persuaded by another bank, also linked to an insurance enterprise: this is a case where two or three insurers appear as co-insurers of the same risk for reasons other than underwriting policies. The concept of co-insurance is expressly regulated by the ICA, which states that: 'If more than one insurance contract have been concluded by joint agreement, with or without a common insurance co-ordinator (leader), each insurer shall be proportionally liable for the insured amount ("co-insurance").'

323. A specific type of co-insurance used for several years was steadily tendered by three insurance undertakings, then belonging to the public sector, so that the involved undertakings were deemed to be the sole co-insurers against fire risks, with each of them undertaking the same percentage of the risk in each individual contract. This represented a case of pooling under the form of co-insurance and was terminated in 1990. Today, there is pooling for specific motor vehicle coverage, while for large industrial risks, there is no national pooling.

Part IX. Taxation of Insurance and Risk Management

Chapter 1. General Remarks

324. Insurance is taxed on several levels: (a) the insurance company is subject to direct taxation, i.e., income tax; (b) premiums are subject to indirect taxation, i.e., turnover tax; (c) the insurance money is subject to stamp duty.

Chapter 2. Taxation of the Insurance Undertakings and Insurance Intermediaries

325. The income of insurance companies is subject to taxation according to the rules on taxation of incorporations. Income comprises premiums earned in Greece by virtue of insurance covering insureds residing in or risks situated in Greece, irrespective of where the insurance contract was concluded. Income deriving from a policy issued in Greece by a foreign insurer in favour of an insured not residing in the country is not subject to domestic taxation.

Profits consist of the aggregate income of the insurance company after expenses, and compulsory reserves are deducted. Reserves are calculated on aggregate net premiums, i.e., after reinsurance premiums are deducted. Life and non-life technical provisions of insurance companies are formed according to actuarial principles. Expenses incurred by the insurance company during the fiscal year are deducted in accordance with the provisions of the Income Tax Code (Law 4172/2013). Distributed profits are additionally taxed as income of the shareholders. The dividend tax is withheld by the corporation paying the dividend, and it is paid to the state.

326. Policies sold by EU insurance companies by way of freedom of services regime aimed to cover risks situated in Greece are subject to Greek indirect taxation. A domestic tax representative must be appointed to ensure compliance with indirect taxation requirements in Greece. However, the obligation to pay the provided indirect tax is not dependent upon the appointment of such a representative.

327. Non-Greek insurance companies established in Greece are taxed on profits derived from policies covering risks situated in Greece.

The income of insurance intermediaries from their insurance business is taxed according to the common rules on income taxation. Their share of the premium is subject to withholding income tax. The insurance company withholds and pays the same to the Tax Authority.

Chapter 3. Taxation of Premiums

328. The insurance business is not subject to value added tax but is subject to the turnover tax imposed on aggregate premiums. The turnover tax, which is called 'premium tax', is paid to the fiscal Authority by the insurance company and constitutes a burden on the contracting party, who pays it upon payment of the premium. Aggregate premiums include premiums due but not received, premiums appearing on policies, as well as any sum paid by way of supplement by the insured to the insurer and is taken into account when calculating the formation of technical provisions covering the risk, whether such payments constitute, for example, remuneration to agents or brokers, or otherwise. Eventual discounts to insureds cannot be deducted from the aggregate premiums. Reinsurance premiums are not subject to turnover tax because the respective sums are included in the insurance premiums, which have already been taxed.

329. Some groups of insurance are exempted from turnover tax. Marine transport insurance, the insurance of imported or exported cargo or aircraft, hull and aviation insurance, as well as life insurance with a duration longer than ten years are all such types of insurance. The insurance of tobacco leaves is partly exempted from turnover tax.

330. Tax rates differ among the various insurance classes: fire premiums are taxed at a 20% rate; life insurance premiums at 4% unless, as already mentioned above, the contract is concluded for more than ten years, in which case premiums are not subject to taxation. The remaining classes are taxed at a 15% rate. In contracts covering risks of more than one class, the fiscal Authority determines the rate by splitting the premium after estimating the importance of each risk in the specific case and the probability of its occurrence.

It should be noted that claim settlement carried out by Greek or foreign insurance companies established in Greece through a branch or agency is not subject to value added or turnover tax, while other quasi-insurance activities, such as remuneration for back-office services, are subject to indirect taxation. The distinction between these two kinds of business is not always easy.

Chapter 4. Taxation of the Insured

331. Further to the indirect taxation of premiums, taxation is imposed on the insureds, in connection with both payment of the premium and receipt of the insurance money.

Non-life insurance premiums are deducted from the income of the insured when these are not included in the price of the property or merchandise insured. Premiums for group life insurance of employees of corporations are regarded as expenses and are deducted up to an amount of EUR 1,500 per employee.

The insurance money may be considered as taxable income of the insured. We must distinguish between individuals and corporations insured, as well as between life and non-life insurance. The insurance money paid to individuals as compensation for losses caused by the insured risk is not taxable, but amounts which eventually exceed the actual loss are taxable, irrespective of the fact that such payments could be regarded as void as a product of the insured's unjust enrichment. If the insurance money is paid to a designated third beneficiary or if it is paid to the heirs, a payable donation or inheritance tax, as the case may be, is imposed. There is a withholding of 15% on the return of the technical provisions' investment.

Stamp duty of 2.4% is imposed upon payment of the insurance money.

Chapter 5. Risk Management

332. In Greece, the term 'risk management' is taken to connote activities which aim at investigating, assessing and reducing the risk. There are specific studies in Greece on this topic and local methodology, as a supplement to the international guidelines on risk management.

Risk management is taught in business courses, and insurance company managers or executives, practising risk management, usually receive relative training. Foreign reinsurers often assist in risk management of their reinsured, while non-Greek insurers established in Greece usually receive such guidance from their seat. Over the past years, there have been attempts to analyse the local factors pertaining to risk management, partly in view of the particularities of risks located in Greece but mainly because of the fact that insurance is a developing area and risk management constitutes an important aid in extending insurance to risks not customarily covered. Notably, all insurance companies operating in Greece have recently been required to get accustomed to the provisions of the Solvency II EU Directive and the special risk management issues involved therein.

333. The principal function of risk management is to identify the risks and to suggest alternative ways for dealing with them. It should be noted that in Greece, the level of risks' prevention is not that high, and consequently, there is ample space for development in this field.

Within this framework, the various safety measures and safety devices and equipment are deemed to form a unified total, where information relating to the various risks is collected.

Risk management entails two levels: risk analysis and risk valuation. On both levels, the standard methods of international practices are used.

Selected Bibliography

This section contains only monographs by Greek authors published in Greek.

Argyriades, A., U. Chatzinikolaou-Agelides & L. Skalides. *Basic Elements of Insurance Law*. 5th edn. Thessaloniki: Sakkoulas Publications, 2007.

Athanasiades, I. *Private Insurance Contract*. Athens: Sakkoulas Publications, 2006.

Bechlivanis, A. *The Pre-contractual Duty of Information*. Athens: Sakkoulas Publications, 2008.

Behri-Kehagioglou, G. *Collective Insurance*. Athens: Sakkoulas Publications, 2010.

Chatzigagios, T. *Private Insurance Law*. Thessaloniki: Anikoula Publications, 2009.

Chatzinikolaou-Agelides, U. *Insurance Contract*. Thessaloniki: Sakkoulas Publications, 2000.

Chatzinikolaou-Agelides, U. *Liability Insurance*. Athens: Sakkoulas Publications, 1986.

Chatzinikolaou-Agelides, U. *Private Insurance Law*. 6th edn. Thessaloniki: Sakkoulas Publications, 2020.

Christodoulou, D. *The Pre-contractual Duty of Information in Private Insurance Law*. Athens: Sakkoulas Publications, 2005.

Christodoulou, D. *Reinsurance: The Institution and the Contract*. Athens: Nomiki Bibliothiki, 2020.

Georgakopoulos, L. *Commercial Law Handbook*. Vol. II, issue 2. 2nd edn. Athens: Sakkoulas Publications, 2002.

Kakavitsas, J. *Basic Principles of Reinsurance*. Athens: Forum Publications, 1993.

Kalantzis, A. *Private Insurance Law as it Appears in Case Law*. Athens: Nomiki Bibliothiki, 1988.

Kiantos, B. *Cargo Marine Insurance*. Vol. III. Thessaloniki: Sakkoulas Publications, 1972–1982.

Kiantos, B. *Insurance Law*. 9th edn. Thessaloniki: Sakkoulas Publications, 2005.

Kiantos, B. *The Insurable Risk in Fire Insurance*. Thessaloniki: Unpublished doctoral dissertation, Aristotle University of Thessaloniki, 1961.

Koutsoyannis, I. *The Insured Interest*. Athens: P.D. Sakellariou Editions, 1928.

Kritikos, A. *Compensation in Case of Road Accidents*. 5th edn. Athens: Sakkoulas Publications, 2019.

Kyriakoulakos, P. *The Contractual Evaluation of the Insured Interest*. Athens: Faculty of Law at the University of Athens, 1967.

Maniatopoulos, I. *Insurance Subrogation*. Athens: (n.p.,), 1955.

Metallinos, A. *International Private Insurance Law*. Athens: Sakkoulas Publications, 1997.

Selected Bibliography

Papapolitis, N. *Shipowner Liability Insurance*. Athens: (n.p.), 1955.
Passias, I. *Life Insurance*. Athens: I. Zacharopoulos, 1936.
Perdikas, P. Commercial Law Manual. Vol. II, 3rd edn. Athens: (n.p.), 1963.
Rokas, I. *Insurance Law: From Theory to Practice*. 5th edn. Athens: Nomiki Bibliothiki, 2020.
Rokas, I. *Insurance Code, Basic Greek Legislation of Private Insurance Explanatory Notes and Critical Comments*. 3rd edn. Athens: Sakkoulas Publications, 2012.
Rokas, I. *Insurance intermediation, Distribution of Insurance Products after the Implementation of the IDD – Critical Remarks/Comments per Article of L. 4583/ 2018*. Athens: Sakkoulas Publications, 2019.
Rokas, I. *On the Control and Supervision of Private Insurance*. Athens: (n.p.), 1978.
Rokas, I. *Private Insurance Law in Case Law*. Athens: (n.p.), 1979.
Rokas, I. *Private Insurance, Part A' – The Contractual Insurance Law & Part B' – The Enterprise*. 13th edn. Athens: Sakkoulas Publications, 2021.
Rokas, I. *Solvency II Supervision of (Re)insurance Companies – Critical Remarks/ Comments per Article of L. 4364/2016*. Athens: Sakkoulas Publications, 2016.
Rokas, I. *Towards a Modern Insurance Law, 1984–2006, Legal Opinions/Legal Studies*. Athens: Sakkoulas Publications, 2007.
Rokas, K. *Abandonment in Marine Insurance Law*. Athens: I. Zacharopoulos, 1951.
Rokas, K. *Life Insurance*. Athens: Konstantinidis - Tsigaridi, 1936.
Rokas, K. *Private Insurance Law*. Athens: (n.p.), 1974.
Rokas, K. *Third-Party Life Insurance*. Athens: Papanikolaou, 1936.
Sinanioti-Maroudi, A. *Insurance Law*. 2nd edn. Athens: Nomiki Bibliothiki, 2017.
Skouloudes, Z. *Private Insurance Law*. 3rd edn. Athens: Sakkoulas Publications, 1996.
Tsagaris, E. *Marine Insurance*. Athens: Sakkoulas Publications, 1954.
Tsagaris, E. *The Code of Commercial Law and Special Commercial Legislation*. Piraeus: Proteus,, 1955.
Tsagaris, E. *The Greek Private Maritime Code: An Article by Article Analysis*, II vols. Athens: Proteus, 1958.
Tsirintanis, A. *Insurance 'For Whom It May Concern'*. Athens: To Nomikón, 1942.
Tsirintanis, A. *Under-Insurance*. Athens: (n.p.), 1931.
Tsirintanis, A. (Tsatsos, D.). *Lectures on Insurance Law*. Athens: Sakkoulas Publications, 1959.

Index

The numbers here refer to paragraph numbers.

Index

www.ingramcontent.com/pod-product-compliance
Ingram Content Group UK Ltd.
Pitfield, Milton Keynes, MK11 3LW, UK
UKHW020145290926
15471UKWH00004B/710

9 789403 547916